CULTURES OF THE WORLD
Latvia

Cavendish Square
New York

Published in 2019 by Cavendish Square Publishing, LLC
243 5th Avenue, Suite 136, New York, NY 10016

Library of Congress Cataloging-in-Publication Data

Names: Barlas, Robert, author. | Wong, Winnie, author. | Duling, Kaitlyn, author.
Title: Latvia / Robert Barlas, Winnie Wong, and Kaitlyn Duling.
Description: Third edition. | New York : Cavendish Square, [2019] |
Series: Cultures of the world | Includes bibliographical references and index. |
Audience: Grades 6 and up.
Identifiers: LCCN 2018046332 (print) | LCCN 2018046530 (ebook) |
ISBN 9781502647375 (ebook) | ISBN 9781502647368 (library bound)
Subjects: LCSH: Latvia--Juvenile literature.
Classification: LCC DK504.56 (ebook) | LCC DK504.56 .B37 2020 (print) |
DDC 947.96--dc23
LC record available at https://lccn.loc.gov/2018046332

Editorial Director: David McNamara
Editor: Kristen Susienka
Copy Editor: Nathan Heidelberger
Associate Art Director: Alan Sliwinski
Designer: Jessica Nevins
Production Coordinator: Karol Szymczuk
Photo Research: J8 Media

CONTENTS

LATVIA TODAY

SOME HAVE CALLED IT "EUROPE'S BEST-KEPT SECRET." OTHERS remember it for its Soviet past. Today, with a rich history, a bustling capital city, an overall population of about two million, and a wealth of opportunity, Latvia is not to be ignored. The year 2018 marked the one hundredth anniversary of Latvia's first independence. The event was observed with huge celebrations in Riga, the capital, as well as additional festivities all across the nation. It is clear that Latvians have much to be proud of, and even more to look forward to in the future.

BUILDING A FUTURE

A country can leave its past behind, or it can learn and build from it. Latvia has chosen to do the latter. At various stages in this country's history, it was inhabited by tribes, invaded and occupied by neighboring powers, and marked by the presence of Germany, Poland, Sweden, and Russia. The country has survived two world wars and fifty years of Soviet rule, hidden away behind the Iron Curtain that threatened not only its long-held traditions but also the well-being of those who lived within the

Soviet Union's borders. Today, the country is a brilliant mix of multiple European ethnicities, but it is also figuring out how to become one Latvian people. This effort presents many challenges. From differences in language and customs to using the rhetoric of ethnic fighting to influence political campaigns, Latvia is right in the thick of some difficult issues. Through it all, however, the people of Latvia refuse to give up.

Latvia has had to claim its own independence more than once, but during the 1990s, as it was breaking away from the USSR, the country became known as "a nation that sings." The "singing revolution" brought to light the Latvians' desire and will to be an independent people, free from Soviet rule. The "singing revolution" phrase refers to the peaceful fight for freedom that included Estonia, Latvia, and Lithuania, commonly known today as the Baltic states. But Latvia has long been home to a culture of folk music based on poems called *dainas*. These dainas are based in pre-Christian legends and themes, and began over one thousand years ago. In the 1980s, Latvia once again proved that it is the singing nation, joining together with its Baltic neighbor-states to sing at rallies and protests in support of independence.

THE NATION TODAY

Today, Latvia is well into its third decade of independence. What a ride it has been! Since 1991, the country has been forced to take a hard look at itself, its people, and its values. What sort of country does it want to be? How should it function? Who should be in charge? What has emerged out of the ashes of the former Soviet state is a country that recognizes its past while leaning into its future.

During the Soviet period, schools, along with nearly every other aspect of everyday life, were run by the state.

The wild, forested land of Latvia is populated by a variety of forest animals. Latvia's gentle plains are covered in trees and plants. These areas offer beautiful landscapes for all to enjoy, and 10 percent of the country's total land is protected by the government. Though timber and woodworking are important parts of the Latvian economy, the citizens have decided that they care deeply about sustainable farming and want to see these forests last into the far future, right along with the industries. This is just one of the ways in which Latvia is bouncing back from its industrial past and working to improve the environment. Plagued by air pollution and water pollution that are holdovers from the Soviet years, the country is working to "clean up its act" in terms of pollution. It is also helping to address the climate change that is wreaking havoc on so many parts of the world.

Today, Latvia has emerged as a bustling, twenty-first-century nation with plenty to offer.

Latvia is a place of both the urban and rural, but the distinctions aren't too sharp. The capital city, Riga, holds about 640,000 residents, a number that has been on a slight decline in recent years. A gorgeous place that holds so much history, it is home to museums, concert halls, universities, shops, and churches. Some might say that it is the heartbeat of Latvia. Its airport is the largest in the Baltic states, and it receives over one million visitors each year, many of whom are tourists who have come to enjoy Latvia's multiple seasons, pleasant outdoors, and rich history. With a distinct lack of arable land, the rural side of Latvia is not a farmer's paradise, but it is home to a robust woodworking industry. Outside of Riga and a handful of smaller cities, Latvia is dotted with towns, roads, train tracks, lakes, and rivers. It is a relatively peaceful place, especially since it has gained independence and taken control of its own narrative.

A visit to Riga, Latvia, is not quite like a visit to other major European cities such as Paris or Rome. It has its own flavor and history entirely, touched by other countries and cultures over thousands of years. To know Latvia is to know a people who are committed to moving forward united, not only within the country but also within the European Union and NATO (North Atlantic Treaty Organization), of which Latvia is a part. In some areas, stepping into Latvia feels like stepping back in time, when folk traditions, songs, and rituals played a large part in everyday life. Other parts feel distinctly urban, with all the hustle and bustle of a twenty-first-century city, and all the technology, business, and politics that comes with it.

Moving further into the twenty-first century, Latvia will continue to chart its own course as a sovereign Baltic nation. We can be sure that it will look to some elements of its past for inspiration and will hold on to other parts as a warning. Through the numerous challenges it has endured and opportunities it has taken up, Latvia has emerged as a peaceful yet spirited player on the world stage, just about ready to step into its shining moment and share its full potential with the world.

Riga's Old Town has vibrantly colored houses, cobbled streets, and incredible architecture.

GEOGRAPHY

Latvia's capital city, Riga, has become quite a tourist destination over the last few decades.

1

WHEN YOU THINK OF EUROPE, YOU might imagine rich natural resources, towering mountains, or rushing rivers. Latvia has none of those things, but it still carries its own unique, tranquil beauty. Dominated by flat land and blanketed in forests, its geography is serene, picturesque, and beautiful. Small bodies of water dot the landscape. What the country lacks in majestic views or landscapes primed for adventure, it more than makes up for in its relaxed, easygoing land that is perfect for travelers driving across its plains, as well as residents who call this magical, forested country "home."

"If you look at our culture, and even going deeper into the folklore, you can see all the environmental wisdom expressed there in that culture."
—Valdis Abols, filmmaker

Latvia borders Estonia, Russia, Belarus, and Lithuania, as well as the Baltic Sea.

Latvia is a very flat, forested country. There are only a few hills. The highest point is Gaizinkalns. It rises 1,024 feet (312 meters). It is a great place to ski!

Latvia is located in Eastern Europe. The country covers an area of 24,938 square miles (64,589 square kilometers), which is slightly larger than the US state of West Virginia, or the combined territories of Belgium and the Netherlands in Europe.

Latvia lies across the Baltic Sea from Sweden; south of Finland and Estonia; north of Poland, Lithuania, and Belarus; and west of Russia. Its western boundary runs along the shores of the Baltic Sea and the Gulf of Riga.

Latvia is situated on the northern edge of the European Plain, a relatively flat landscape with a few gently rolling hills. The characteristics of the land were formed during the Ice Age, when large masses of ice moved across the area. The Baltic Sea coast of Latvia consists of a coastal plain 308 miles (496 kilometers) long. The flatness of this area, a former sea bottom, is occasionally broken by coastal ridges, but plains are the predominant landform throughout the country.

Latvia's lake district is one of many unique regions within the country.

UNIQUE REGIONS

Latvia is divided into five major regions—Zemgale, Kurzeme, Vidzeme, Latgale, and the capital area of Riga.

The region of Zemgale is bisected by the Zemgale Plain and is dominated by the Lielupe River. The plain is a depository of sandy clay and is the most fertile grain-producing area of the country. Hilly areas can be found to the west and in the southeastern part of the region, especially at its borders with the Daugava, Latvia's principal river.

To the west, the region of Kurzeme is more undulating than Zemgale. The hills of Vidzeme to the northeast and Latgale to the east are interspersed with lowland areas, river valleys, lakes, marshes, and boglands. The soil of Vidzeme and Latgale is poorer and less suited to crop farming than the soil in Zemgale

and Kurzeme. Latgale is crisscrossed by streams and interconnected by lakes with numerous islets, and it is often referred to as Latvia's lake district.

Tourists and locals alike take advantage of the high points in Latvia, such as this popular ski slope.

MOUNTAINS AND LAKES

Latvia is a very low country. The average elevation is only 285 feet (87 meters) above sea level, whereas its highest point, called Gaizinkalns, located in the uplands of central Vidzeme, is only 1,024 feet (312 m).

There are about 2,250 lakes in Latvia. The largest is Lake Lubans, covering an area of 31.4 square miles (81.3 sq km). The deepest is Lake Dridzis at 214 feet (65 m). Both lakes are located in the Latgale region in the east.

RIVERS AND STREAMS

Latvia has numerous rivers and streams, some twelve thousand in all, but only seventeen are longer than 60 miles (97 km). The four major rivers in Latvia are the Daugava, Lielupe, Venta, and Gauja.

The Daugava, which begins in central Russia, is the largest river, flowing through Belarus before entering Latvia to empty into the Gulf of Riga. The total length of the Daugava is 632 miles (1,017 km). Outside of Latvia, it is referred to as the Western Dvina.

The Venta originates in Lithuania. It is renowned for its waterfall, called the Rumba, at the city of Kuldiga. The river mouth forms a natural harbor for oceangoing ships at Ventspils, where it flows into the Baltic Sea.

Latvians are lucky enough to experience all four seasons, including colorful fall.

A COUNTRY OF SEASONS

Despite being situated quite far north, Latvia's climate is relatively temperate, with mild winters and moderately warm summers. Spring comes in late March, when flooding is common due to melting snow and the break-up of river ice. The mild, warm summer weather arrives in June and lasts until September. This is the season of the heaviest rainfall, with frequent thunderstorms and precipitation. Typically, July is the warmest month of the year, with an average temperature of 62.4 degrees Fahrenheit (16.9 degrees Celsius).

During the fall months, there is frost, high humidity, and fog, particularly in coastal areas. Winter sets in around November. January is the coldest month, with an average temperature of 23.5°F (–4.7°C). Most snowfall occurs between January and March. Despite the small size of the country, there are marked differences in climate from west to east in Latvia.

PLANTS AND ANIMALS

There are three main plant habitats in Latvia: coniferous and broadleaf forests, swampy marshes, and grass-covered meadows. As of 2015, forests—more than half of which are pinewood—cover approximately 54 percent of the country.

In Latvia there are thousands of different animal species, including rodents such as squirrels and beavers, and carnivores such as wolves, foxes, lynx, and martens. Many of Latvia's animals can also be found in other countries in the region—wild boar, elk, red deer, and the swamp turtle. The American mink and the Norwegian rat were accidentally introduced into Latvia. Other

Beavers build sturdy dams on the country's many waterways.

nonnative animals include the jenot (a kind of raccoon dog related to foxes), fallow deer, and wild rabbits.

There are more than 350 species of birds in Latvia. These include storks, common waterfowl, turtle and rock doves, several species of grouse, the barn owl, the house swallow, the greenish warbler, and even the Arctic loon. The white wagtail is the national bird of Latvia.

URBAN LIVING

Most of Latvia's present-day urban centers evolved from early settlements near rivers and other sites along trade routes. The cities developed their own local traditions, religious character, and political systems, which were tempered over the years by the various occupying powers—Poland, Sweden, Germany,

The sun sets over the city of Daugavpils, Latvia.

The official flag of Latvia, which is deep red with a horizontal white stripe, has been in use since the year 1280.

and Russia. The major cities in Latvia today are Ventspils, Riga, Daugavpils, Liepaja, Jelgava, Jurmala, and Rezekne.

RIGA Riga is the capital of Latvia. It is situated on the Daugava River estuary, where it flows into the Baltic Sea.

Riga was an important trading post during the Viking Age. It was officially established as a city by the German Sword Brothers, who built fortresses along the river. The Citadel of Riga was built in the seventeenth century, and Riga soon became one of the strongest fortresses and shipping ports on the eastern coast of the Baltic Sea.

During the 1930s, Riga was referred to as "the Paris of the north," with its grand streets and broad boulevards. The old historic part of the city, known as the Old Town (or Vecriga), has been preserved and protected over the centuries, and most of the area has been restored to its original state with narrow cobblestone streets, richly decorated doors, tile roofs, and churches.

The focal point of the modern city of Riga is the Liberty Monument, where Latvians gather to show their love and devotion to their homeland, and to remember the despair and hope of the long years of the Soviet occupation.

DAUGAVPILS Daugavpils, the second-largest city in Latvia, is situated in the southeast on the Daugava River. The first written record of Daugavpils is from 1275, but archaeological digs show that the area has been inhabited since the Stone Age. Daugavpils is the administrative center of the Latgale region and is an important transportation junction in eastern Latvia. Due to its proximity to Russia, Belarus, and Lithuania, Daugavpils has become an important center of trade and commerce.

Daugavpils is also noted for its rich and varied cultural and educational activities. Russian, Belarusian, Jewish, Lithuanian, Polish, and many other societies do their best to preserve and support their own traditions. Daugavpils University is noted as a national training center for teachers, while scientists from Latvia and abroad study at the Latgale Research Institute.

LIEPAJA Liepaja is located on Lake Liepaja, where its waters enter the Baltic Sea. It has a population of more than eighty-five thousand and has been inhabited since the ninth century. Liepaja has been part of many different countries since 1625, including Sweden, Prussia, the Russian Empire, and the former Soviet Union.

One of the city's major features is its artificial harbor, which was built between 1697 and 1703. It was deepened in the middle of the nineteenth century to remain ice-free during the cold winter months. As a gateway to the West, the entry became an important communications center in 1869, when it was linked with Copenhagen, Denmark, by an undersea cable.

During the Soviet occupation, access to Liepaja was restricted because of the large Russian naval base there. Liepaja is noted for its excellent port facilities, as well as being an important Latvian industrial center.

JELGAVA Jelgava is situated on the banks of the Lielupe River, which serves as a major transportation route between Riga and Lithuania. It was officially founded in 1573 but was mentioned in historic documents dating back to 1265.

Jelgava Palace is now home to the Latvian Agricultural University.

Ventspils has twice featured the Cow Parade exhibition of public art.

As the capital of the Zemgale region, Jelgava first developed as an active trade and commerce center. During the eighteenth century it was also a printing center. The first Latvian newspaper, *Latviesu Avizes*, was printed here and elsewhere, as were half of all Latvian-language books. Today, main industries in Jelgava include technology, motor mechanics, agriculture, carpentry, and veterinary medicine. Jelgava's most important landmark is the grand Baroque-style Jelgava Palace, which was designed by Italian architect Francesco Bartolomeo Rastrelli. It took over thirty years to complete. It is located on the site of a castle built by the Livonian Order in 1265, near the Lielupe River. The original palace was destroyed during World War I, but it was rebuilt during Latvia's first period of independence.

VENTSPILS Ventspils is located on the shores of the Baltic Sea at the mouth of the Venta River in western Latvia. The city was an important trade and commercial center throughout its history, and the mouth of the Venta was known to navigators as early as the twelfth century. In early times, it was inhabited by the Couronians (or Kurs), then by the Livonian Order in the thirteenth century.

Ventspils became a shipbuilding center during and after the Duchy of Courland (1561—1795). During the seventeenth century it was an important port of the Duchy of Courland, which included Kurzeme and Zemgale provinces. The city continues to be a key transportation center, with the port active today. This world-class port is ice-free, and the world's largest tankers and cargo ships can be docked in its deepened shipping canal all year round. Other industries growing in popularity in the city include manufacturing and services. Likewise, tourism has taken off in recent years. In the early 2000s, a major ecological cleanup effort to repair the damage caused from extensive environmental neglect during the Soviet era helped transform Ventspils into a tourist destination, and its reputation as such continues today. Each year, around 110,000 people visit the city to take in its sights for a week or just a few days.

When imagining the vast, forested country of Latvia, one might think of the land as desolate or cold, dry, and unforgiving. On the contrary, Latvia is a country of differentiated seasons, numerous small bodies of water, and a great public appreciation for the land. All forests in Latvia are publicly accessible, and berry picking and mushroom hunting are popular pastimes. For Latvians, the country's geographical features are its strength and its heritage. Those in Latvia care deeply about the plains, forests, wildlife, cities, and other features of their small but mighty country.

INTERNET LINKS

http://www.entergauja.com/en
Here, you can learn all about Gauja National Park.

http://www.liveriga.com/en
Check out this site to learn all about the city of Riga.

http://www.lob.lv/en
This organization is focused on bird and nature conservation in Latvia.

HISTORY

The Old Town district in Riga features cobblestone streets and buildings from the medieval era.

2

"Just as one calls
into the forest, so it
echoes back."
−Latvian proverb

LATVIA HAS A LONG AND FASCINATING history. Though people have been living in the Latvian region for thousands of years, the country has changed hands several times. Invasions, takeovers, and trades are all parts of Latvia's history. Today, it enjoys independence, though its time as a wholly independent country has been relatively short. The bulk of Latvia's history takes place in the hundreds of years prior to the Soviet takeover and subsequent collapse of the Soviet Union. Through all of the trials and triumphs of its long life, the region remains connected to its ancient past and continues to learn from the modern-day events it has endured.

FIRST PEOPLE

The first inhabitants of Latvia were nomadic tribes that migrated along the Baltic Sea after the last ice age some ten thousand years ago. In

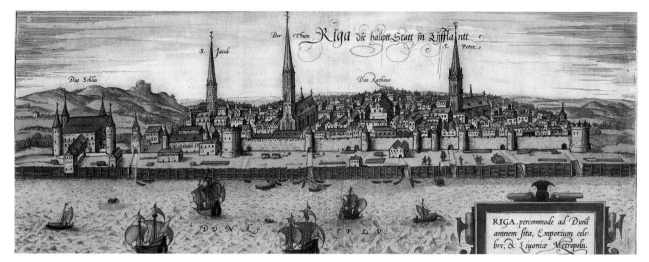

Over the centuries, Latvia's shores have endured numerous settlers and invaders. This drawing shows Riga, Latvia's capital, in the 1600s.

2000 BCE, a new group of settlers—the proto-Balts, or early Baltic people—came from the south and established permanent settlements on the eastern shore of the Baltic Sea in the territory known today as Latvia. The Finnic people—early ancestors of the Estonians, Finns, and Livonians—were already in these lands before the arrival of the Balts. Latvia became famous for its amber, and a trading network was established from Scandinavia along the Daugava River. A trade route to Constantinople and Persia was established as well. Around 900 CE, the Balts began to establish individual tribal cultures—Couronians, Semigallians, Selonians, and Letgallians. In the 1100s and 1200s, the Couronians, who had settled along the coast of the Baltic, became known as the "Baltic Vikings." Similar to the Scandinavian Vikings, they traveled far to raid and loot, as well as trade. The other tribes, located farther inland, were peace-loving farmers.

The Germans were the first to succeed in invading Latvia. The first German merchants arrived in the second half of the twelfth century. In 1198, Pope Innocent III proclaimed the Baltic Crusade. His aim was to cut off the northern trade routes of Constantinople as well as convert the people of the Baltic region to Roman Catholicism. The crusade ended a century later, when the last Latvian tribe was subjugated. Riga was founded by the Germanic bishop Albert I of Livonia in 1201, and within one hundred years it joined the Hansa League, forming important cultural and economic relationships with all countries of Europe.

GERMAN INFLUENCE

In 1237, the Latvians, including tribes in what is now known as Estonia, were under complete German domination, and the area was united by the Teutonic Knights into a state known as the Confederation of Livonia. For the next 270 years, Latvians gradually turned into serfs under these German-speaking knights, merchants, and church officials.

The local German nobility, who were landowners, asked Poland for protection when Ivan the Terrible of Russia invaded Latvia during the Livonian War of 1558 to 1583. The Muscovites (as the Russians were called at that time) were not completely successful in conquering Livonia, as they faced opposition from the Poles. Ivan's armies were eventually driven out. In return, the greater part of Latvia was incorporated into the Kingdom of Poland, while the western part of Latvia became the autonomous Duchy of Courland under Poland's protection.

For the next two hundred years, the Duchy of Courland remained an independent naval and commercial power in northern Europe with its own army, navy, and, until 1795, its own monetary system.

THE SWEDES AND RUSSIANS

Latvia continued to be a political football for many years. During the Polish-Swedish War from 1600 to 1629, Sweden acquired the region of Vidzeme and Riga. The Swedish king, Gustavus Adolphus, brought about immediate administrative and judicial reforms and made great efforts to strengthen Lutheranism and foster education. Taxation was based on the amount of property a person owned. Land surveys and censuses produced the first detailed maps of Latvia. Schools and courts were established for the native population. Historians often refer to this period as the "good old Swedish Era." However, local nobility resisted these Swedish reforms and kept most of the ethnic Latvian population as serfs.

The Swedes ruled Vidzeme and Riga until 1710. Riga, the largest city in Sweden's empire, was an important link to major states and cultures throughout

Why is Latvia considered a "Baltic" country? The word is geopolitical in nature. It came into use after World War I to describe the countries on the eastern coast of the Baltic Sea. Today, Estonia, Lithuania, and Latvia are the "Baltic" states. They each regained their independence after the fall of the Soviet Union and have retained unique identities and histories.

Saint Peter's Church in Riga opened in 1746.

Europe. Vidzeme supplied the Swedish kingdom with wheat and was known as "Sweden's bread basket."

During the Great Northern War, from 1700 to 1721, Russia defeated Sweden and expanded its borders into Livonia, of which sections of Latvia were a part. Later, between 1778 and 1795, Russia annexed eastern Poland and brought Latgale, Zemgale, and Kurzeme under Russian control. The Swedish judicial reforms were thrown out, and the conditions of Latvian peasants deteriorated once more. Their compulsory labor was increased to six days a week, while the landed gentries were exempt from taxation. During this period, many beautiful castles were built on the estates of the Baltic barons. To support their lavish lifestyle, landlords demanded higher taxes from the peasants.

The economic and social domination of the Latvian people reached its lowest point during Polish and Russian domination. Landlords acquired more and more land and forced excessive taxes on the peasants.

Marija Simanska (1922–1995) was a well-known Latvian chemist. In 1952, she was one of the first three Soviet women to receive a doctorate in chemistry. She went on to be an inventor, researcher, writer, and one of the most prolific scientists in Latvian history.

A NATIONAL AWAKENING

The Age of Enlightenment, a period when a belief developed in the power of reason, science, and the possibility of human change for the better, spread through Europe in the eighteenth century, but it was slow in coming to Latvia. Although a tract advocating the complete emancipation of the peasants was published in the late 1700s, the ethnic German gentries strongly opposed any reforms and were powerful enough to resist change for a long time. Beginning in 1818, a series of laws were passed in which the peasants were given personal freedom and limited freedom of movement. Some Latvians succeeded in getting basic schooling for their children. However, most Latvians were still dependent on their landlords for their livelihood. A major breakthrough came in 1868 when a law was passed to eliminate mandatory service to manors. This forced the gentry to hire labor and to sell an ever-increasing amount of land to their former tenants to obtain cash.

NATIONALIST FIGUREHEADS

The most prominent leaders of the first National Awakening Movement (1850–1870) were Krisjanis Barons, a leading scholar of folk poetry, and Krisjanis Valdemars, who established a maritime school of navigation and shipping business. Juris Alunans was the first widely published poet, and later, Atis Kronvalds became a fiery orator who criticized German domination of social and economic life in Latvia. Karlis Baumanis was the organizer of the first National Song Festival in 1873 and author of the national anthem of Latvia. These poets and writers modernized the Latvian language, making it suitable for literature as well as contemporary science and business. When government censorship was relaxed, they published  *the first Latvian-language newspapers. They fought to establish schools for the non-German population. In Riga, Latvians established numerous cultural organizations, such as the Song and Dance Celebration, which brings together choirs from all over the Latvian-speaking territory.*

RUSSIA TAKES OVER

As a result of finally being able to buy their own land, a much larger number of Latvians became landowners in the latter part of the nineteenth century and so began to have the financial resources to educate their children and take part in social and cultural activities. The University of Tartu in Estonia was the nearest institution of higher education, and by the 1850s it was attracting significant numbers of Latvian students. With this growth of education, Latvians became reacquainted with their history and their ethnic heritage, which led in turn to a growth in national identity.

Ironically, soon after this reawakening of national feeling, Latvia was undergoing a major wave of Russification—Russians only in all official positions, the Russian language mandatory in schools and in all institutions, and enforcement of the Russian Orthodox faith. The revolution of 1905 in Russia was a turning point that inspired the Latvians to take up arms against their German landlords and Russian rulers. Although this revolt was put down mercilessly by czarist troops, the stage was set for Latvia's war of independence thirteen years later.

Red Army troops enter the city of Riga in 1919.

AN INDEPENDENT LATVIA

On November 18, 1918, Latvians declared national independence and formed a provisional government. The war of independence had begun. Fighting continued for the next two years against the leftist social democrats known as the Bolsheviks in Russia, who—despite leader Vladimir Lenin's promises—wanted to incorporate Latvia into the new Soviet Russia, and also against the Germans, who had similar plans for Latvia.

By 1920, the Germans and the Bolsheviks were both defeated by the Latvian national armed forces. Latvia signed a peace treaty with the Soviets in which the Soviet Union recognized "unconditionally the independence and sovereignty of Latvia and decline[d], voluntary and for all times, all claims on the Latvian people and territory which formerly belonged to Russia." Latvia was established as a democratic republic, and the first period of Latvia's real political independence began.

Latvia's democratic, parliamentary government was recognized by all the world powers. On September 22, 1921, an independent Latvia was admitted to the League of Nations, a precursor to the present-day United Nations. For just over a decade, the country enjoyed its newfound peace.

From 1934 to 1940, Latvia's democratic government was briefly interrupted in an authoritarian coup led by Prime Minister Karlis Ulmanis. He dissolved the

Saeima (parliament) and established executive non-parliamentary authoritarian rule. Key government offices, communications, and transportation facilities were removed. The incumbent president, Alberts Kviesis, served out the rest of his term until 1936, after which Ulmanis merged the offices of president and prime minister. When the Soviets reoccupied Latvia in 1940, Ulmanis was forced to resign.

In this October 1944 photo, Latvian soldiers from the Red Army walk through Riga.

EARLY INDEPENDENCE

Following independence, laws were passed concerning the redistribution of land, and the number of landowning farmers increased by nearly 100 percent. Several hundred ethnic German families had owned more than half of the farmlands in Latvia. These were taken back and redistributed to volunteers in Latvia's war for independence. The first decade of independence also saw the rebuilding of the economy. Farming shifted from grain to dairy production, and food exports became a stable source of national income. Most factory equipment had been evacuated to Russia during World War I, and never returned. New

factories were established to produce consumer goods. Forest products were also profitable exports. The State Electrotechnical Factory began to produce radios and telephone equipment. A hydroelectric generating station supplied 40 percent of Latvia's electric power.

AN UNEXPECTED ULTIMATUM

However, Latvia's independence did not last. In 1939, the Soviet Union and Nazi Germany signed the Molotov-Ribbentrop Pact, which included a secret protocol that consigned independent Latvia, along with Estonia, Lithuania, and Finland, to the Soviet sphere of influence.

In October 1939, Latvia received an ultimatum from Moscow demanding the immediate free entry of Soviet troops into Latvia's territory. The Red Army crossed the Latvian border the following day, and in June 1940, a Soviet-installed government took power. During the next twelve months, more than thirty-two thousand people were deported or executed, and entire families were sent to labor camps in Siberia. About twenty thousand Latvian men were drafted into the Red Army.

THE SOVIET YEARS

Soviet subjugation of Latvia was interrupted by fighting between the Germans and the Soviets during World War II. By 1941, the German Nazis had occupied all of Latvia, exacting their own terror on the populace. About seventy thousand Latvian Jews (nearly the entire Jewish population) were brutally murdered between August and November that year. Their bodies were buried in mass graves, such as the one near Rumbula. About eighteen thousand non-Jewish Latvians also perished.

Initially, Latvians hoped that the Germans would reinstate Latvia's independence, but this did not happen. Several nationalist organizations took root, with participants including former members of parliament and other political leaders, as well as ordinary citizens. They promoted a unified, democratic society. One of the defining leaders of the nationalist push

was Konstantins Cakste. He, along with other distinguished leaders, created the Latvian Central Council, an underground government. Cakste was a politician and the son of Latvia's first president. His workings within the underground Latvian government, however, were discovered, and he was arrested. He was sent to Germany, where he eventually died in Stutthof concentration camp in 1945.

Soviet soldiers cross a river on the way to Riga in 1944.

As World War II dragged on, Nazi Germany began to suffer regular defeats when fighting Soviet troops on the eastern front. From 1944 to 1945, Latvia was once again reoccupied by the Soviet Union. This time, Russian dominance would last for nearly fifty years and bring with it new waves of terror and deportations. Armed resistance against the Russian occupation lasted until 1956, when it was finally crushed, and all symbols of Latvia's independence were outlawed or altered. Russian was imposed as the official language, farm owners and their families were deported, and their properties were taken over by the government. Factories, too, were now owned by the state. Moreover, a large number of Russians, Ukrainians, and Belarusians were moved to Latvia between 1944 and 1991. In 1959, the Latvian communist government led by Eduards Berklavs attempted to slow the immigration of Russians into Latvia. He was quickly removed from power and relocated to Russia, while many other Latvians, communist and noncommunist alike, lost their jobs and were persecuted by the Soviet government. People lost their rights to freedom of speech, freedom of assembly, and freedom of religious worship. Even owning a banned book or distributing a handwritten political statement were sufficient reasons for arrest and imprisonment in a labor camp.

For the next fifty years, the seat of government and the real power was in Moscow, and Latvia was subjected to a totalitarian way of life where power belonged entirely to the Communist Party of the Soviet Union. Private ownership was prohibited. The state controlled every aspect of an individual's life—from cradle to grave.

Prisoners in this Soviet labor camp were outfitted with identical uniforms and haircuts.

Children attended state-run kindergartens and state-run schools later on. They had to join the Young Pioneers—a state-run organization for young people where control could be maintained over the activities of members and where ongoing political and social indoctrination could be conducted. Later, if they wished to study at a university, they would have to join the Communist Youth Organization (Komsomol).

LIVING IN THE SOVIET STATE

With private property abolished, most city inhabitants were forced to live in apartments that belonged to the state. These tended to be small and cramped, with several separate families living in one apartment, sharing a kitchen and bathroom. The rent was set at a fixed rate, but the government had the power to raise it at its will.

In the countryside, family farms were liquidated and replaced by state-controlled collective farms. If a farm was larger than 20 acres (8 hectares), its owner and his family were classified as "kulaks," or prosperous. More than ten thousand of these people, about half of them children, were deported to Siberia. Pride in work and in one's surroundings disappeared as personal freedom of movement was curtailed. Civil liberties ceased to exist, and arrests, interrogations, and deportations were common.

ENACTING ISOLATIONISM

By the 1960s, the Soviet Union and the countries allied with it were absolutely cut off from the outside world. This means no communication existed with the West, and news from other parts of the world was not available, except when it suited the government.

The desire of the populace to regain independence was silenced by the state rule of the Communist Party and the KGB, its intelligence and internal security agency. Moreover, religious and human rights activists were routinely arrested and consigned to prison camps in the Soviet Union. Until the late 1980s, the campaign for Latvia's independence in the international political arena was mostly carried on by the over 120,000 Latvian exiles in the West who had fled the country in 1944 and 1945. They maintained contacts with dissidents in Latvia and publicized their activities in the world media.

Some displaced Latvian families, such as these children picking cotton in Mississippi, were brought to the United States in 1948.

INDEPENDENCE—AGAIN

Latvia's third National Awakening began with a demonstration in 1987 in defiance of local authorities. It was held at the Liberty Monument in Riga to commemorate the victims of the 1941 Soviet deportation. After this, with each subsequent rally and demonstration, the old rules established by the Soviet regime began to fall. Even the communist government of Soviet Latvia joined the movement, declaring Latvian to be the official language of the

The peaceful Baltic Way demonstration took place on August 23, 1989.

republic, and reinstating the national flag after a mammoth demonstration of three hundred thousand people in July 1988. On August 23, 1989, after fifty years of the Molotov-Ribbentrop Pact, nonformal organizations sprang up everywhere, uniting to form a single political organization, the Popular Front (Tautas Fronte). The Popular Front joined similar organizations in Estonia and Lithuania to organize the largest-ever Baltic demonstration—the "Baltic Way." A 373-mile- (600 km) long human chain, made up of nearly two million people from the three Baltic states—Estonia, Latvia, and Lithuania—stretched from Tallinn in Estonia, through Riga, to Vilnius in Lithuania.

In 1990, for the first time ever under Soviet rule, voters had a choice of two political groups: the Communist Party, which favored remaining in the Soviet Union, and the Popular Front, which desired independence. The Popular Front won two-thirds of the vote, and on May 4, 1990, the newly elected parliament voted to restore Latvia's prewar status as an independent republic with a transitional period. During the crackdown on Lithuanian and Latvian independence in January 1991, Soviet OMON (Otryad Militsii Osobogo Naznacheniya, a special-purpose police unit) troops killed five people in Riga.

But by August 21, after the collapse of a coup in Moscow, Latvia succeeded in the complete reinstatement of its independence. After a constitutional convention that renewed the democratic system established in 1918, the first free parliamentary elections were held in 1993. The prewar currency, the Latvian lat, again became the official currency. In 1994, Latvian president Guntis Ulmanis and his Russian counterpart, Boris Yeltsin, signed an agreement to withdraw all Russian troops from Latvian soil. Following the renewed independence, Latvia quickly returned to the international milieu. It became a member of the Organization for Security and Co-operation in Europe (OSCE) and the United Nations (UN) in 1991. In 1998, Latvia began negotiations to join the European Union (EU) and NATO, and became a member of both in 2004. Its pro-market, pro—free trade policies enabled Latvia to become the EU's fastest-growing economy from 2004 through 2006.

The world economic crisis in 2008 caused Latvia's economy to collapse. Output fell more than 10 percent in the last quarter that year, and many people

Following independence, Latvia spent much of the 1990s attempting to repair Latvian-Russian relations within the country. Today, some tensions continue, especially as Russia looks toward expansion in the twenty-first century.

Riot police were present at this 2009 protest against the Latvian government, a response to the deepening economic crisis.

found themselves without work. Public anger spilled into the streets in January 2009 as scores of protesters clashed with police when they tried to storm the parliament. More than forty people were injured in Latvia's worst riots since the country gained independence from the Soviet Union.

Following the riots, the Latvian economy continued to falter, and the country found itself with the highest jobless rate in the European Union, at 20 percent. Following the inability of the government to agree on austerity measures to fix the economy, Valdis Dombrovskis formed a new center-right government, Union of Greens and Farmers, and was elected prime minister. A member of the same party, Andris Berzins, was elected president by the parliament in June 2011. Berzins defeated Valdis Zatlers, who was hoping to fight against corruption. Dombrovskis served from 2009 to 2014.

MOVING FORWARD

The next few years were up and down for Latvia. The year 2013 saw the collapse of a major supermarket in Riga, and fifty-four people were killed in the accident. Prime Minister Dombrovskis took full responsibility and resigned. This opened the door for a new candidate, who would be the first-ever female prime minister in Latvia—Laimdota Straujuma. She ran as a member of the conservative Unity Party. Under Straujuma's leadership, Latvia joined the Eurozone and adopted the Euro as their currency, replacing the lat.

The year 2014 was a tense time for the Baltic states. Over the late winter, Russia used its military power to seize Crimea, a small peninsula that was historically part of Ukraine. These actions were heavily condemned by countries across the world, who expressed concerns about human rights abuses in Crimea. Sanctions were imposed against Russian officials. NATO sought to assure Latvians that they would be protected in the event of a Russian attack or annexation, and began conducting major military drills in the Baltic states in 2015.

In late 2015, Laimdota Straujuma resigned as prime minister, due in part to coalition clashes over the federal budget and the number of EU migrants legally allowed to enter the country. The year 2016 saw Maris Kucinskis elected prime minister as head of Straujuma's coalition.

Today, the independent Latvia is still a very young country—not even thirty years old in its current form. It has worked hard to join friendly forces with other nations, and is now a member of the European Union, the Eurozone, the Council of Europe, the United Nations, and NATO. Citizens are working hard to guarantee a good quality of life to all people within the country's borders and are in the midst of defining the country's new cultural values, such as environmental sustainability. The year 2017 saw the country ranked fourteenth on the Ease of Doing Business Index, a project of the World Bank Group that tracks property rights protections and better business regulations. In 2018, Latvia was ranked tenth on the Climate Change Performance Index. These are both signs that the country is in a period of economic growth, as well as a period of evolving and progressing priorities, values, and strengths.

Laimdota Straujuma made history as Latvia's first female prime minister. Here she is in Brussels, Belgium, in 2015.

INTERNET LINKS

https://eudocs.lib.byu.edu/index.php/History_of_Latvia:_Primary_Documents
If you want to read original documents related to Latvian history, this site has an impressive collection.

http://www.latvia.eu/history/history-latvia-timeline
This handy timeline hits all the main points in Latvian history, both ancient and modern.

http://100in1.lv/en/routes/one-day-of-latvian-history
This website includes a map, list, and pictures for those who are planning a trip to Latvia that focuses on the country's history.

GOVERNMENT

This is the Saeima building in Riga. Latvia's representatives meet here. The word "saeima" means a "gathering, meeting, or council."

3

CROSS THE WORLD, NATIONS HAVE unique and varied ways of running their countries. Borders show where a country is. A country's government shapes how the country runs. It creates laws and rules, regulates businesses, and even defines how citizens will work together to help one another, such as through the distribution of tax dollars. Those who want to truly know a country should take a hard look at its government. The structure, elections, and running of the government can give a person insight into the values and priorities in a certain state. For many years, Latvia was controlled by various outside forces. Since the early 1990s, the country has formed and run its own government. Today, we see the results of many years of thinking, planning, and building that have gone into the newly independent government system in Latvia.

"Education in secondary schools in the Latvian language will ensure equal opportunities for all young people to get a good education and make a living in Latvia, to study and work here."
—President Raimonds Vejonis

Latvia is an independent democratic republic. The constitution provides for separation of legislative, executive, and judicial powers; for the separation of church and state; for freedom of the press, conscience, speech, and assembly; and for equal rights for all citizens, including cultural autonomy for ethnic minorities.

The major political parties in the Saeima, or parliament, include Harmony (Saskana); Who Owns the State? (Kam pieder valsts?); New Conservative Party (Jauna konservativa partija); Development/For! (Attistibai/Par!); National Alliance (Nacionala Apvientba); and Union of Greens and Farmers (Zalo un Zemnieku Savientba) as of 2018.

Political advertisements dot the cityscape of Riga during election seasons.

LATVIA'S GOVERNMENT

Ultimate power is vested in a single-chamber parliament, the Saeima, which has one hundred elected deputies who serve a term of four years. The deputies have control over domestic legislation and international treaties, determine the size of the armed forces, and have veto power over the national budget, which is proposed by the cabinet.

Latvia has a small but mighty military, which includes land, naval, and air forces. Here, a military parade takes place in Riga in 2017.

The president is elected by the Saeima for a term of four years and a maximum of two consecutive terms. The president can initiate legislation, appoint diplomatic representatives, and is the commander in chief of the armed forces. He has the power to initiate the dissolution of the Saeima, but the Saeima has the power to dismiss the president by a two-thirds vote.

The prime minister is proposed by the president, but must be approved by parliament. The prime minister has the power to choose the members of the cabinet, who have voting rights on matters in their areas of responsibility. Latvia's cabinet oversees a number of ministries, such as Social Welfare, Defense, Foreign Affairs, Education and Science, Justice, and Environment.

The judicial structure consists of township courts, justices of the peace, juvenile courts, district courts, a court of appeals, and the supreme court.

CURRENT TENSIONS

The main current international political issue is Latvia's heightened political and military tensions with its Russian neighbors. In recent years, Russia has become more aggressive, especially in its 2014 annexation of Crimea. In 2015, Raimonds Vejonis was selected as the Latvian president. Vejonis previously

In Latvia, the parliamentary group is referred to as the Saeima. In the United States, it is called Congress. In the United Kingdom, it is called Parliament. The word "Saeima" means a council, meeting, or gathering. The Saeima is a large council that gathers together to make decisions on behalf of the Latvian people.

On March 14, 2014, Vladimir Putin (*seated, second from right*) signed the treaty of the annexation of Crimea.

Today, some refugees have been able to find safety and stability in Latvia.

held the position of defense minister, which was seen as an advantage in regards to Latvia's relationship with Russia. Though relations are not expected to reach levels of military action, the Latvians of today and the future will need to figure out how to both respect ethnic Russians living within Latvia's borders and continue to assert the country's independence.

IMMIGRATION

The issue of acquiring Latvian citizenship through naturalization for foreigners was one of the most difficult matters for the government in the years following independence. In the early 1990s, one-third of the people were not citizens; their ethnicity was mainly Russian (63 percent of all noncitizens), followed by Belarusian (12 percent), and Ukrainian (8 percent). The Latvian government wants to ensure that ethnic Latvian control is maintained but also offers citizenship to the various non-Latvian groups that reside there. To acquire citizenship, a person must have lived in Latvia for five years, must pass a test about the constitution, prove that they have a legal source of income, and pass a basic-level Latvian language examination. Today, about 62 percent of residents are ethnic Latvians, while 25 percent are Russian, and small percentages are Belarusian (3.3 percent), Ukrainian (2.2 percent), Polish (2.1 percent), and Lithuanian (1.2 percent).

Naturalization increased dramatically when Latvia joined the European Union in 2004. By 2009, about half of the former noncitizens had naturalized, but there were still about 238,000 noncitizen permanent residents of Latvia, or 11 percent of the population. The Latvian government provides ethnic minorities—Russian, Polish, Jewish, Ukrainian, Estonian, Lithuanian, Belarusian, and Roma—with an opportunity to study in their native languages while also learning the Latvian language. Latvian remains the official language of Latvia.

GOVERNMENT COALITIONS

In the past, as a level of cynicism developed in the years following independence, participation in the political process by the Latvian people declined. There were many political parties, and no distinction among them was clearly visible. Each parliamentary election brought about six to eight parties into parliament, ranging from the nationalist For Fatherland and Freedom to the Russian-speaking Human Rights Party. This is because Latvia has a unique rule. Unlike the United States Senate or House of Representatives, the Latvian parliament cannot be ruled by one party. The parties have to figure out how to work together. However, over the years, government coalitions have varied in stability, some lasting several years, others less than a year. Today, even though the politicians may have figured out how to coexist, they are still determining how to work well together.

Nils Usakovs is the first mayor of Riga of Russian descent since 1991.

GROWING POLITICS

In the years following independence, public impatience for the economic and social benefits of reform was rising, but official corruption was not yet under complete control. Transparency of government decisions was often low, leading to public distrust.

After the 2006 election, the new government moved swiftly to remove the head of the Anti-Corruption Bureau, Aleksejs Loskutovs, which led to a mass protest called the "Umbrella Revolution," because it took place on a rainy day. Removal of Loskutovs was temporarily delayed, but it was nevertheless completed several months later.

The municipal elections of 2009 resulted in a new shift in Latvian politics. In Riga, the winner was the Harmony Party, representing mainly Russian-speaking voters; the mayor of Riga, Nils Usakovs, is an ethnic Russian. Harmony chose the First Party, a pro-business, Christian-values party, as its coalition partner.

This unification, however, was not evident in the rest of the country. As Latvia climbed out of the financial struggles that occurred from 2008 to 2011, a center-right government was formed, and the pro-Russian Harmony Party was excluded from the coalition government. This exclusion has continued over the past few years, especially amid concern about Russia's growing expansionism.

LEADERSHIP

Maris Kucinskis became prime minister of Latvia in 2016.

In April 2015, incumbent president Andris Berzins announced that he would not seek a second term. After elections were held later that year in parliament, Raimonds Vejonis won and became the ninth president of Latvia. He is a member of the Green Party, which is an arm of the Union of Greens and Farmers. Vejonis is committed to the environment, having served as both the minister of environmental protection and as minister of the environment. He also served as the minister of defense of Latvia in 2014. He stated that he would like to improve relations with Russia, but that its military presence in Ukraine was unacceptable and was contributing to tension.

Maris Kucinskis was appointed by the parliament as prime minister of Latvia in February 2016. He replaced Laimdota Straujuma in the role. Straujuma, who took office in 2014, had announced her resignation in late 2015 amid disputes with her coalition. Economic woes, teacher strikes, and a flood of European migrants all caused strife between Straujuma and the ruling coalition. Upon leaving, she recommended Rihards Kozlovskis as her successor, but he declined the role.

MILITARY

Latvia bases its defense concept on four pillars: a collective defense as a member of NATO, professional armed forces, support and coordination with civil society, and international military cooperation.

Currently the National Armed Forces of Latvia include the Ground Forces, the Navy, the Latvian Air Force, the Border Guard, and the Latvian Home Guard, called Latvijas Zemessardze.

At the age of eighteen, young men and women may volunteer for military service. Conscription to the armed forces was abolished in 2007. Under current law, every Latvian citizen is entitled to serve in the armed forces. The National Armed Forces (NAF) exists to protect Latvia from potential threats to its national security and from organized crime. Another involvement of the NAF is participation in international peacekeeping operations.

The Home Guard is under the direct authority of the president. The Security Service consists of a special battalion of soldiers whose job is to fight against terrorists and to provide escorts for visiting dignitaries.

When Latvia gained its independence, it had the unique opportunity to design its own form of government. Like many other countries, Latvia ended up with a president, a prime minister, and a parliamentary group. One facet that makes Latvia's government particularly distinct (and different from the United States in particular) is that no one party is allowed to take full political power. Regardless of who wins the elections, members of different parties are forced to work together to create coalition governments. While this certainly isn't the most efficient way to make changes within a country, it does leave room for many different voices to be heard, and it restricts abuses of power that are more likely to occur in partisan systems.

Over the years, leadership has changed hands from various parties, and different worldviews have waxed and waned in popularity. In the coming decade, it will be interesting to watch and see which issues come to the forefront for Latvians. Immigration, education, tax reform, and other hot-button topics are already on the table. As it has in the past, the political system in Latvia will surely continue to evolve and grow as generations age and beliefs, values, and issues change.

Latvian land forces are currently deployed on several peacekeeping missions.

INTERNET LINKS

https://www.nationalgeographic.com/archaeology-and-history/magazine/2017/09-10/russian-revolution-history-lenin
An article from National Geographic's *History* magazine explains how the USSR, of which Latvia was once a part, first formed.

https://www.president.lv/en
This is the official website of Latvia's president.

http://www.saeima.lv/en
This is the home page of Latvia's parliament.

ECONOMY

4

PRIOR TO 1991, LATVIA'S INDUSTRIES were controlled by the Soviet state. For over fifty years, the people of Latvia did not experience a free market. Everything was centralized—from collective farms to state ownership of the factories and centralized planning that dictated what was produced and sold. After Latvia gained its independence, its new leaders had a huge challenge ahead of them. How could they take the country from a centralized economy controlled by outside forces to a free-market style? The free-market style is enjoyed by most countries around the world, including the United States. Though the free market is not a new type of economy, it was relatively new to Latvia's leaders and citizens. They were forced to quickly learn and adapt.

"The financial woes have been successfully resolved, but economic, social and political challenges remain." —Aldis Austers for *Intereconomics*

During the changeover, major industries, which had been totally dependent on raw materials and energy from the former Soviet Union, were privatized, upgraded, and restructured to become competitive with those in Western economies. By 1996, more than 93 percent of state-owned enterprises had been privatized through the Latvian Privatization Agency. By the end of the 1990s, the private sector produced almost 90 percent of the country's gross domestic product (GDP). Latvia's economy grew more than 10 percent (GDP) during 2006 and 2007, but it experienced a recession in 2008 as a result of a global financial crisis, an imbalance between its imports and exports, inflation, and also insufficient banking regulation during the rapid growth of real estate values in the early twenty-first century. Luckily, the country was able to pull itself out of the crisis through financial discipline. Between 2011 and 2013, the economy recovered, and by 2014 the country's national credit rating reached an appropriate level. Today, the credit rating remains stable. In 2016, Latvia's government had one of the lowest debts relative to its GDP among European Union member states. At the same time, unemployment continues to decrease

Forestry is a bustling and lucrative industry in Latvia.

and the banks have gotten back on track. The European Commission and World Bank predict that the country's economy will grow in the coming years.

MAKING MONEY

Latvia's economy is based on services, industry, forest products, and agriculture. Transit trade through three ice-free harbors (Riga, Ventspils, and Liepaja) makes up a significant portion of the service sector. Industries include processed foods, processed wood products, textiles, processed metals, pharmaceuticals, railroad cars, synthetic fibers, and electronics. The service industry includes retail and wholesale trade, real estate, business activities, transportation, storage, and communication.

Hydroelectric power is produced in Latvia by three hydroelectric-generating stations located on the Daugava River, two on the Aiviekste River, and nine on the Gauja River. Some of Latvia's electricity supply comes from Estonia,

In 2016, the GDP in Latvia was worth $27.68 billion US. This put it solidly between its Baltic neighbors. Lithuania's GDP was a little higher, while Estonia's was somewhat less.

Peat harvests provide an important source of energy to many parts of the world.

A combine works a field in Bauska, Latvia.

Lithuania, and Russia. Latvia has no oil or natural gas deposits, so gas is imported from Russia. Peat is still used as an energy source and is also exported.

Latvia's chief exports are wood products and agricultural products. Most of Latvia's exports are to other European Union countries.

Imports from European Union countries constitute the largest overall percentage and include machinery and equipment, motor vehicles, consumer goods, fuels, and mineral and chemical products.

GOING TO WORK

In Latvia, the employment code, which has been updated on a semiregular basis since 1992, regulates all employment legislations. A minimum wage has been set by the law. The typical workweek in industry is forty hours in a five-day week. In risky and taxing industries, days last closer to seven hours instead of eight. Vacations may range from two weeks to one month. As in many other countries, there are laws regarding overtime, sick leave, and mandatory breaks. These laws ensure that workers are not exploited or treated unreasonably.

TAXES

With the regaining of independence, Latvia had to introduce its own system of revenue generation. The main sources of revenue were taxes—mainly a social welfare tax in the form of a flat-rate payroll tax. This method of taxation was first introduced by Estonia in 1994, and the other Baltic states, including Latvia, were quick to adopt it. For many years, Latvians were taxed a flat rate of 23 percent on all income, no matter how much money they made during the year. This means that low-wage and high-wage earners were all taxed about one-quarter of their income. In 2018, the country moved to increase revenue by introducing changes to the tax code. Today, individual earners are taxed progressively on a scale between 20 percent and 31.4 percent, depending on how much they make during the year. The country also introduced a higher corporate income tax in 2018.

GETTING AROUND

As in many other parts of the world, owning a car is the aim of every Latvian family. As a result, the number of cars on the roads is growing at a rapid rate. The European Union has contributed large subsidies to rebuild and improve roads and other infrastructure that declined after decades of neglect during the Soviet period. As roads have improved, more and more Latvians have purchased new cars. Volkswagen and Audi are the most popular brands in the country. According to 2012 reports, a higher share of cars are registered "in good working condition," which means that Latvians are replacing their old vehicles at higher rates.

There are three main seaports that can accommodate oceangoing vessels in Latvia—Ventspils, Riga, and Liepaja. The main activity in these ports is the transshipment of cargo from countries formerly part of the Soviet Union to

Developed infrastructure allows for ease of transport in Riga.

countries in the West. A regular ferry service from Riga to Stockholm leaves daily from both destination ports. The journey takes about seventeen hours each way. A number of small fishing ports dot the coast of the Gulf of Riga.

The airports in Riga, Ventspils, and Liepaja handle local and international passenger and cargo traffic. Trains link Latvia to Germany, Ukraine, Russia, Lithuania, and Estonia. Within Latvia, traveling by bus is inexpensive and often faster than trains. Riga also has a commuter rail that provides extensive service.

Latvian Railway's international trains travel from Latvia to Lithuania, Estonia, Russia, Belarus, Ukraine, and Poland.

Economists remain guardedly hopeful about the future state of Latvia's economy. Just as the country was working to rebuild as an independent, capitalist economy in the 1990s, the 2008 global economic recession sent Latvia's federal debt into a tailspin, ballooned the unemployment rate, and put everyone on rocky financial ground. However, with the help of its international allies, Latvia has been able to rebuild. Though no one would refer to this state as an economic superpower, its slow growth remained steady in the years since the recession, and the country is now in a much more stable condition. According to economists, the introduction of a new tax code should put both businesses and consumers on track for an even healthier and more prosperous economy in the coming years.

Latvia's railway system includes both domestic and international routes.

INTERNET LINKS

https://europa.eu/european-union/about-eu/money/euro_en
This site has everything you need to know about the euro.

http://www.latvia.eu/economy
Learn about the country's economy straight from its federal website.

https://www.worldbank.org
The World Bank is an institution that provides loans and monetary assistance. It helped Latvia during the 2008 recession.

ENVIRONMENT

The rich forests of Latvia are an important national resource.

5

EVEN THOUGH EARTH IS INHABITED by everyone who lives on it, we do not work communally to protect and respect its environment. Every country has its own environmental policy. States, cities, and even small towns have adopted their own environmental regulations in an effort to keep the planet clean and healthy. Each country has its own environmental history, too, and Latvia's is a tough one.

ENVIRONMENTAL HISTORY

Like most former Soviet republics, Latvia suffers from decades of environmental mismanagement as a result of rapid buildup of heavily polluting industries, as well as the past military activities of the USSR, which were not environmentally friendly. In the late 1980s, however, Latvian leaders began to talk about protecting the environment. This was also fuel for the independence movement. The Latvian environmental movement grew from grassroots to full-fledged activism when the Soviet government tried to construct a dam on the Daugava River in 1988. Plans were canceled following protests, which further emboldened the environmental activists. Around this time, the environmental groups began to merge with pro-independence groups, working together to collectively

Since the Soviet years, new landfills have opened in Latvia. This one is in Latvia's Rezekne county.

oppose not only Soviet environmental practices but the Soviet regime as a whole.

Since regaining independence, Latvia's economy has shifted to service industries rather than manufacturing (though a manufacturing sector remains), and this has brought benefits to the environment. The government has designated new nature reserves and parks, and also has ratified several international agreements on reducing air, water, and land pollution. The country retains a minister for environmental protection in its federal government. Today, wetlands, endangered species, and forested areas are being protected. Sustainable energy consumption tops the list of current environmental priorities. In 2017, Latvia was ranked third in the European Union for highest share of renewable energy in overall consumption. Most of their renewable energy—97 percent—is produced through hydropower plants, while the other 3 percent is produced by wind turbines and biomass. In 2010, Latvia's parliament approved the Sustainable Development Strategy 2030, a twenty-year plan that sets goals for conservation, greenhouse gas emissions, natural resource use, and recycled waste. Today, Latvia's environmental policy prioritizes air quality, water management, and waste management.

SEWAGE SYSTEM AND DRINKING WATER

The first water supply device was built in Riga in 1620. Water was pumped from an open reservoir and ran through wooden pipes to pools and directly to homes of noblemen. By the nineteenth century, however, industrial and agricultural waste was polluting the Daugava River, from which water was being drawn. Before long, the river's water was no longer safe to drink. After 1904, new water sources had to be found outside Riga. New wells were drilled to meet industrial demands and the needs of an expanding population. The Daugava station in Riga treats and supplies half the drinking water for the city of Riga. The rest comes from groundwater pumped from more than three hundred drilled wells. Almost half of Latvia's untreated water contains bacteria of unacceptable safety levels. Additionally, levels of nitrogen and phosphorus have recently begun to trend upwards, owing to agricultural activity near wells, as well as human activities. Water pollution in wells is often due to placement near cattle barns, restrooms, and other areas. The country continues to struggle with and prioritize water protection at the same time. Luckily, Latvia does not have the challenge of water scarcity. Freshwater resources exceed the needs of the population.

During the Soviet era, all sewage was discharged into reservoirs adjacent to the district of Riga. Some treatment plants were built in the postwar period. In the mid-1980s, about 7 percent of sewage was treated biologically, and 22 percent mechanically. After independence in 1991, Latvia implemented a large-scale program to treat its sewage waste. A pressure collector system, large pumping stations, and a biological wastewater treatment plant were installed.

Today, Latvia's wastewater treatment facilities are much better equipped to handle the country's population. In 2010, the Riga Wastewater Treatment Plant increased its plant capacity in order to comply with EU standards. Since then, the plants in Riga and across the country have remained in compliance.

Though the tap water is safe, many Latvian drink bottled or filtered water for its taste.

WASTE

Under Soviet domination, little attention was paid to the environment in each town. Occupied Latvia invested heavily in the manufacturing industry but neglected treating hazardous waste. This resulted in the pollution of lakes, rivers, and the Baltic Sea. The Daugava River and the Gulf of Riga reached dangerous levels of pollution from industrial and agricultural chemicals. In 2009, Latvia's first hazardous waste disposal landfill began operation in Zebrene, in the Dobele region. It was designed to handle 9,000 tons (8,164 metric tons) of communal and industrial waste each year. Today, the state operates a hazardous waste temporary storage facility in Gardene and a waste incineration facility in Olaine, in addition to the landfill at Zebrene. Latvia has also opened ten new non-hazardous waste disposal sites over the last few years, reducing environmental and human health risks.

THE AIR LATVIANS BREATHE

Emissions of polluting substances in the air promote environmental problems such as acidification, formation of ground-level ozone, and accumulation of hazardous chemical substances in living organisms. Air pollution is most noticeable in major urban areas where industries are concentrated. Since 1997, the government of Latvia has laid down restrictions on emissions for certain sectors where solvents are used and for emissions of volatile organic compounds from oil depots, fuel filling stations, and especially incineration facilities. Latvia's effort to decrease pollution has effectively reduced the emissions of acidified substances, deposits of sulfur, and nitrogen over time. However, a high percentage of Latvian citizens are still exposed to air pollution

Like many developed countries, Latvia struggles with pervasive air pollution.

on a daily basis. From 2011 to 2015, nearly 90 percent of urban dwellers in Latvia were exposed to pollution concentrations above EU standards. In 2018, the European Court of Auditors reported that Latvian citizens had higher numbers of "lost years of healthy life from ambient air pollution" than residents of both China and India, countries that are often cited for their unhealthy air pollution levels.

While the country is not a leader in the global environmental movement, it does work hard to comply with EU regulations and international agreements such as the Kyoto Protocol, which it joined in 2002, and the United Nations Framework Convention on Climate Change, where it has been a member since 1995. In 2018, Latvia ranked tenth on the international Climate Change Performance Index. Emissions, renewable energy, energy use, and climate policy are the four categories that are measured for the index. In 2017, lawmakers ratified the Paris Climate Agreement, committing to a collective target for cutting greenhouse gas emissions by 2030. The document is legally binding and is set in order to help reduce global warming.

CLIMATE

In Latvia, the effects of global climate change are felt a little more each year. Heavy rainfall, increased storm frequency, and hail have been affecting the country over the last decade. According to official records, damage caused by heavy rainfall and lightning strikes has increased over the past few years as well, especially when it comes to real estate and machinery. In 2013, a record was set for the largest insurance claim for damages caused by natural disasters in Latvia. The damage was due to heavy rainfall.

Despite the presence of hail, strong winds, and storms, Latvia continues to be a country full of vibrant wildlife, both on land and in the water. Some animals are common in Latvia but rarely seen across Europe, such as the black stork, Eurasian beaver, and lesser spotted eagle. The diversity of plant and animal species is due in part to the nation's vast areas of protected land. Marshes, woodlands, lakes, rivers, forests, meadows, groves, and beaches all spread seamlessly across Latvia's vast, untouched plains. Unlike many

Latvia is home to many different nature reserves and parks, like Kemeri National Park, shown here.

countries that contain long coasts, Latvia's has remained unmarred by resorts and restaurants. The white sand beaches, though not of the tropical sort, are publicly accessible and often uncrowded.

BIODIVERSITY

While about half of Latvia is covered in forests, a full 5 percent is marked by marshes and mires. These areas host over twenty protected bird species, ten protected types of insect, and one very rare snail. Teici State Reserve is the largest protected mire in the Baltic region. It is full of swamps, bog pools, and lakes, as well as the largest concentration of premigratory cranes in the country.

Latvia is known for its protected nature and wildlife areas. In fact, 10 percent of Latvia lies within a protected nature area. The very first protected area, Moricsala Nature Reserve, is an island in Usma Lake. It was designated as such

FOREST REGULATION

A little more than half of the land in Latvia is covered by forests, 50 percent of which is state-owned. For their part, the Latvian government regulates and protects the forests with consistency and organization. Harvesting, regeneration, monitoring, and management are regulated through federal legislation. This means that Latvian citizens do not need to worry about their forests disappearing any time soon.

in 1913. For ecotourists, Latvia is a great place to see rare plants and animals, as well as beautiful, untouched land and waters.

When it comes to protecting the environment, Latvia still has a long way to go. The young country is working hard to clean up the mess made in its Soviet past. Air pollution and water pollution continue to plague residents. In 2015, a new Environmental Policy Strategy was adopted, which created a new model for revenue from the natural-resources tax, improved wastewater management standards, and ushered in changes in waste management. The strategy was adopted through 2020, after which time the Latvian government will need to reassess its environmental goals, practices, and policies.

INTERNET LINKS

https://climate.nasa.gov
Here, NASA gives an in-depth look at the ways in which Earth's climate is changing due to global warming.

http://www.latvia.eu/nature/wildlife
Latvia is a country full of different species of animals, plants, and insects. Explore its biodiversity here.

http://www.varam.gov.lv/eng
This state agency covers environmental issues across the country of Latvia.

LATVIANS

Here, traditional dress meets contemporary technology during the Song and Dance Celebration in 2018. These young women are laughing and smiling while taking a photo.

6

T HE TERM "LATVIAN" ENCOMPASSES a wide range of peoples, histories, languages, customs, and experiences. However, over the years, those living in Latvia have had some trouble coming together as a united people. In 1990, everyone had to pull together to achieve independence, but since then, disputes between minority groups have loomed large at times.

Latvia is made up of ethnic Latvians, Russians, and other groups. Most recently, tensions have flared between Latvians and Russians, who feel they are being forced to assimilate to the Latvian way of life through the teaching of Latvian in schools. At stake are questions about equality, assimilation, diversity, and what it means to be Latvian. As years progress, it will be interesting to see what comes of the discussion, and whether the people of Latvia can unite behind common causes.

CITIZENSHIP

The population of Latvia is about 1.94 million. Latvia's ethnic mix is largely a result of postwar immigration, which led to a decline in the share of ethnic Latvians from 77 percent in 1935 to 52 percent in 1989. Since then, the portion of ethnic Latvians has risen to 62 percent, with the remainder made up of a mixture of ethnic groups. Russians make up 25.4 percent.

At one time, there were over one hundred thousand Jews who called Latvia their home. During World War II, that number was drastically lowered due to the Holocaust. Many Jews were killed or forced to leave, while others escaped to different countries. Today, the number of Jews living in Latvia is less than fifteen thousand.

Latvia's city centers are home to high-rise buildings and contemporary architecture.

Minority populations include Belarusians at 3.3 percent, Ukrainians at 2.2 percent, Poles at 2.1 percent, Lithuanians at 1.2 percent, and others at 3.8 percent.

After Latvia regained independence in 1991, citizenship was granted to all pre—World War II citizens and their descendants. Naturalization is relatively easy, requiring five years of residence, a test of basic-level Latvian language, proof of income, and a test on the constitution. After the five years of residency have been completed, it usually takes less than a year for a person to gain Latvian citizenship. Numerous surveys have attempted to find why so many people in Latvia (some 12 percent of the total population) choose to remain noncitizens. Though the percentage has decreased significantly over the years, over two hundred thousand individuals remain noncitizens. The majority are Russian-speaking residents who moved to Latvia during the Soviet era. Reasons vary, but many noncitizens mention ease of travel to Russia as a factor: visas are expensive for citizens of Latvia, while noncitizens pay only a small fee. But Latvian noncitizens cannot vote in Latvian elections or work in civil services. Otherwise, they live life as other residents do, with most of the same rights and responsibilities. When a baby is born in Latvia to noncitizen parents, the parents have the option to request Latvian citizenship for their child. Each year, however, some parents don't request citizenship for their children, so a number of infants are born with noncitizenship status. In 2016, for example, fifty-two newborns in Latvia were classified as noncitizens. In September 2017, President Vejonis attempted to introduce an initiative that would change this policy, but it was defeated in the Saeima.

MINORITY STATUS

RUSSIANS Russians were the largest minority in Latvia after World War I, making up about 10 percent of the population in 1935. Refugees from Russia after the Bolshevik Revolution created a vibrant community in Riga, with a daily newspaper, theater, and many other cultural activities.

By 1935, there were 206,499 Russians in Latvia. Several hundred thousand ethnic Russians entered Latvia immediately after World War II, and a steady stream of immigration continued into the 1980s. By 1989, the number had increased to 905,515. In the years after Latvia regained independence, a wave of Russian emigration began to take place; between 1992 and 1994 some 62,000 returned to Russia. In 2006, about two-fifths of the population in Riga was Russian (42.3 percent), and in the second-largest city, Daugavpils, over half the population (53.3 percent) was Russian. By 2017, the number of Russians living in Riga had fallen to 37.88 percent, with Latvians making up about 44 percent.

Latvian Russians are culturally united by their use of the Russian language, rather than by their nationality. Russian intellectuals have formed a number of organizations to promote Russian culture and education in Latvia. The two main Russian-speaking political parties represented in the national parliament and municipal governments are Harmony and Latvian Russian Union.

The Latvian Russian Cultural Center, founded in 1994, united seven Russian organizations, including the Russian Children's Choir and the Russian Folk Instruments Orchestra.

In a number of "minority" schools in Latvia, the curriculum is taught in Russian, but this has begun to change in recent years. Major language reforms in the education system are making Latvian compulsory for all high-school-aged students. By 2021, all sixteen- to eighteen-year-olds attending public schools in Latvia will be taught only in Latvian, regardless of the school's designation as a minority school. Out of 811 state-funded schools in the country in 2016, ninety-four had teaching in Russian or bilingual education. Soon, they will need to change in order to keep up with the new policies. Discussion of the legislation caused protests in 2018, just as earlier proposed reforms did in 2004. This time, though, the reforms passed.

UKRAINIANS As of 2017, Ukrainians made up 2.2 percent of the population of Latvia. Under 17 percent of them speak Latvian, and most consider Russian their native tongue, rather than Ukrainian.

Russian-speaking students participate in a Russian literature class in Latvia in 2012.

Many Ukrainians in Latvia are former officers from the Soviet army. Most of them have undergone retraining and are employed in other industries, such as transport and oil, and many more are now retired. More than twenty-five thousand Ukrainians left Latvia after the disintegration of the Soviet Union.

POLES Poles have long been residents of Latvia and are considered one of Latvia's traditional minorities. The number of Poles in the country has barely changed in the last one hundred years, including during the Soviet occupation.

Poles living in Latvia have a strong interest in maintaining their culture and Polish identity. Luckily, relations between Latvia and Poland have remained strong, and the two countries are friendly trading partners that also cooperate militarily. In 2006, an intergovernmental agreement on cooperation in education and culture was signed by leaders of the two countries. This has allowed for the regular exchange of students and teachers. Additionally, the Latvian state operates five Polish schools across the country.

LITHUANIANS As of 2017, Lithuanians made up 1.2 percent of Latvia's population. A high percentage of Lithuanians are engaged in farming, and most have integrated into Latvia. More than half of Lithuanians speak Latvian, and there is a high rate of intermarriage. Still, ethnic Lithuanians retain pride in their heritage.

GERMANS Germans in Latvia occupy a special place among the ethnic minority groups, given that settlers of German descent have lived in the Baltic territories since the thirteenth century. Over the centuries up to independence in 1918, they continued to hold the upper levels of authority in the country.

The Germanic influence on Latvian culture remained very strong until Latvia gained its independence in 1918. At that time, many Germans left Latvia, unable to reconcile themselves to the loss of their former privileges and social status. According to the Russian Empire census of 1897, Germans in

Latvia accounted for 6.2 percent of Latvia's population. By 1935, the German population had dropped to half of what it had been at the turn of the century. Since 1959, the number of resident Germans has increased, mainly due to Germans moving to Latvia from Russia. Presently, 0.1 percent of Latvia's population is German.

JEWS Today, the Jewish population in Latvia is very small—between five thousand and fifteen thousand—and mainly concentrated in Riga. Smaller communities are in Daugavpils and Liepaja. Synagogues are found in Riga, Daugavpils, Liepaja, and Rezekne. Children learn both Hebrew and Yiddish in a Jewish school in Riga. A prominent Latvian of Jewish heritage today is Gidon Kremer, an internationally acclaimed violinist.

Latvia is home to many beautiful and historical synagogues. This one is in Riga.

The first Jewish colony in Latvia was established in Piltene in 1571. The Jews contributed to Latvia's development until the Northern War (1700—1721), which greatly reduced Latvia's population. In the eighteenth century, Jews from Prussia reestablished themselves in Latvia and played a significant role in its economy. In independent Latvia, the Jewish community flourished. Jews formed political parties, and some became members of parliament.

Before World War II, there were about eighty-five thousand Jews in Latvia. By the end of the war, more than 90 percent of Latvian Jews had been murdered. Latvian Jews today are the descendants of survivors of Jews who fled to the Soviet Union to escape the Nazi invasion and later returned, or came to Latvia from other parts of the Soviet Union after the war. Those who are not descendants of prewar residents are unable to enjoy full civil rights. During the 1990s, many Jews left for other countries, especially Israel and the United States. The Jewish population in Latvia continues to decline year after year.

SOCIAL STRUCTURE

Until the nineteenth century, the main occupation in Latvia was agriculture. Most Latvians lived in the countryside as peasants, and there were no class distinctions because everyone lived off the land from the labor of their own hands. Those who lived in the towns and cities were small tradesmen, craftsmen, and artisans. The landowners or barons, who were mostly German, held all the power in local municipalities—even the local clergymen were controlled by them.

With the coming of the first National Awakening in the latter half of the nineteenth century, some Latvians became teachers and ministers and moved into positions of power and responsibility. Some rural Latvians moved to the cities and became involved in trade as owners of businesses and of property. With the development of factories at the end of the nineteenth century, an industrial working class of Latvians also developed in the cities.

During the period of Soviet occupation, society was dominated by the Communist Party. After Eduards Berklavs and other "national Communists" were removed from government in 1959, leadership shifted to the Russian governing class, while the Latvian population moved back to a lower level in the social structure.

ACROSS CLASSES

During the years of independence from 1918 to 1941, the typical social classes of a democratic society evolved—farmers, farm laborers, and small tradesmen in the countryside, and entrepreneurs and workers, along with artists, writers, actors, intellectuals, and bureaucrats, in the cities. Social mobility, at that time, depended on education and one's ability to speak German. A middle class formed, which included businesspeople and other professionals. During the Soviet years, most professional positions were filled by Russian immigrants put in place by the state. After regaining independence, the Latvian economy changed, and socioeconomic classes within the society changed as well.

Today, Latvia includes vast amounts of rural areas and small towns, as well as a few midsize cities and one large urban area, Riga. There is a wide range of positions available for the jobseeker, and one is not required to speak German or be a Russian immigrant in order to fill them. However, despite the theoretical freedom of socioeconomic movement that the free market affords its citizens, Latvia has some of the worst economic inequality within the Baltic states.

This inequality is further exasperated by a nearly nonexistent middle class, as well as high rates of poverty. In Latvia, families and individuals tend to fall on the high-earning or low-earning side of the spectrum. This was due, in part, to high taxes, even on wages for low-earners. This created an incentive for informal employment (payment in cash) and underreported wages. The latest tax reforms are attempting to address some of these issues by alleviating the burden on those who earn the least.

Poverty in Latvia is concentrated among the elderly. Twenty-seven percent of those above the age of sixty-five are living in poverty, mainly due to a retirement system that is badly in need of updating. Incidents of poverty are also high among those of working age who are unemployed, since unemployment benefits in the country reduce after only six months and expire completely after nine months. It is likely that new reforms will be introduced in the coming years in order to address these issues.

This horse-drawn hay thrasher gets the job done.

LATVIAN DRESS

Historically, one of the most conspicuous examples of Latvian national identity was the production of fabrics and garments. Fabric was woven in every peasant homestead. During the feudal era, Latvians were forced to wear national dress and forbidden to wear fashionable clothes. The national dress was supposed to be evidence of the wearer's membership in the lower class. Nevertheless, the bright and varied colors of traditional garments livened up the bleak dreariness of their daily lives.

The classic traditional Latvian folk dress, which remained modest, simple, polished, and noble looking throughout time, dates back to two distinct periods. The first lies between the seventh and thirteenth centuries, known as the "ancient dress" period. The second period ran from the eighteenth to nineteenth centuries and established what is known as "ethnic" or "ethnographic dress." Ancient dress was characterized by plain cloth and accessories made from flax, fleece, furs, and leather. Clothing was constructed locally using locally

Children and adults love to dress up in traditional garments.

harvested and hunted sources. Outfits at this time were decorated with bronze jewelry traded from Scandinavia, Russia, and the Middle East.

In the later centuries, clothing styles were influenced by German culture. The bronze jewelry disappeared, and in its place arrived knitted mittens, gloves, and socks. Homespun garments in gray and white with colored accents became very popular. Linen, wool, and fur were used to make men's coats, women's long skirts, and warm shawls. Mittens became a centerpiece and were often given as gifts at weddings or funerals.

Today, you can find both ethnic and ancient forms of dress on display at the Latvian National History Museum. To see reproductions worn in action, you can visit the national Song and Dance Celebration, where choirs, folk groups, dance ensembles, and others dress up in the traditional costumes.

WELL-KNOWN LATVIANS

KRISJANIS VALDEMARS (1825—1891) Krisjanis Valdemars was the leader of the first National Awakening movement. He was one of those responsible for publishing the first newspaper in Latvian from Saint Petersburg, Russia. Valdemars encouraged Latvians to take pride in their language and history. He urged the peasants to buy land and thus gain financial independence. Moreover, he established a maritime school and advised coastal inhabitants to engage themselves in shipping.

ULJANA SEMJONOVA (1952—) Uljana Semjonova was born in Medumi, a village in the Daugavpils district. She grew to an impressive 7 feet (2.13 m) tall. Between the 1970s and 1980s, Semjonova was the world's leading women's basketball player. She won the championships fifteen times in the Soviet Union league and eleven times at the European Champion's Cup. Semjonova is a three-time world champion in female basketball, and she won two Olympic gold medals while playing for the Soviet Union in 1976 and 1980. She never lost a game in an official international competition.

VAIRA VIKE-FREIBERGA (1937—) Vaira Vike was born in Riga. During the Soviet occupation, her family fled the country and became refugees in Germany and later in French Morocco. In 1954, young Vike arrived in Canada. There she earned a bachelor's degree in 1958 and a master's degree in 1960, both in psychology. The same year, Vike married Professor Imants Freibergs. In 1965, she earned a doctorate in experimental psychology.

Vike-Freiberga is proficient in Latvian, English, French, German, and Spanish, and was active in community service, focusing on questions of Latvian identity and culture, and the political future of the Baltic states. In 1998, she was elected professor emeritus at the University of Montreal and returned to Latvia. In October of that year, she was appointed the director of the newly founded Latvian Institute. On June 17, 1999, she was elected president of the Republic of Latvia by the parliament (Saeima). In 2003, she was reelected for a second term of four years, winning eighty-eight votes out of ninety six. She stepped down in 2007 due to the Latvian law that bars presidents from serving more than two consecutive terms. Since leaving office, Vike-Freiberga has become involved in thirty international organizations, including the World Leadership Alliance and the European Council on Foreign Relations. In 2015, she was a member of two groups on European security and defense, and in 2014, she was elected president of the Club de Madrid. She has been awarded nineteen honorary doctorates, published fourteen books, and received other accolades. She remains well respected in Latvia and around the world.

Vaira Vike-Freiberga was the first female president of Latvia.

When saying the word "Latvian," one may be referring to someone who currently lives in Latvia, but that is never the whole story behind a person, family, or group of people. Ethnic Latvians make up more than half of the country's population, and over the years, the numbers of minorities have grown, shrunk, and shifted. On the whole, the population is on the decline, and some strategists are worried about where that will put Latvia in the next few decades. With fewer people, there will be less tax revenue, and fewer people paying into services like health care and taking part in the military. However, as young people move away from home, they usually go to one of two places: Riga or abroad. Young Latvians believe they can find a better, more prosperous life elsewhere. Some are right, while others return home later. No matter their ethnic identification, a child who grows up in Latvia will be forever shaped by his or her homeland.

LATVIA'S FIRST PRIME MINISTER

Karlis Ulmanis (1877–1942) was Latvia's first prime minister and the last before the Soviet occupation in 1940. The youngest of three brothers, he was born and raised on a farm and took up agricultural studies in Germany. Back in Latvia, he was passionate about incorporating modern farming techniques into the dairy and cattle industries. In 1905, he promoted independence from Russia and was sent into exile. He made his way to the United States. From 1907 to 1909 he studied agriculture at the University of Nebraska. After graduating, he relocated to Texas, where he had a dairy farm.

In 1913, Ulmanis was granted amnesty, meaning he could return to his home country. There, he founded the Latvian Farmers Union and became the party's leader. The union was one of several political groupings to voice the idea of an independent Latvia. It finally got the chance to put theory into action in 1918 when representatives of various organizations and parties formed the National Council after World War I. The council proclaimed a sovereign Latvian state and appointed Karlis Ulmanis as the prime minister.

Ulmanis, however, only remained in power until the summer of 1921. When the Latvian war of independence ended in 1920, Latvia was established as a parliamentary democracy, and its very first Saeima was elected. With a new parliament came new prime ministers, but Ulmanis returned to office in 1925, and again in 1931. Each time, he only served for a few months to a year. During this period, the country was finding its post–World War I footing and establishing its young democracy.

In 1934, Ulmanis was again in power. That year, he suspended the constitution and dismissed the Saeima, suspending all political parties. The political party with the largest voter support, the Latvian Social Democratic Workers Party, opposed the coup. He arrested its leaders and other potential political opponents. Ulmanis quickly established political censorship of the mass media and concentrated all power in the hands of the cabinet, headed by himself. The economic policy that Ulmanis then put in place had much in common with that of Franklin D. Roosevelt's New Deal in the United States, resulting in considerable progress in agriculture, successful development of industry, stable government spending, and a relatively high standard of living for the population.

With the occupation of Latvia by the Soviet Union, Ulmanis was deported to Siberia, where he died in a prison camp in 1942. His final resting place remains unknown. His name will be closely tied forever to Latvia's first real period of independence, as he was one of the major forces in achieving democracy, as well as overturning it.

Across the world, and especially in the United States and in Latvia, his memory brings up a mix of feelings and recognitions. The University of Nebraska-Lincoln has long honored him, as he is the only graduate who went on to become the leader of a country. Some historians celebrate Ulmanis as a symbol of early Latvian independence and a positive force within the country during his first term in office. However, others conclude that his authoritarian measures should not be ignored in favor of advantages he brought the country. Nevertheless, he remains an intriguing person with influence on many in Latvia and abroad.

INTERNET LINKS

https://encyclopedia.ushmm.org/content/en/article/introduction-to-the-holocaust
This website, built by the United States Holocaust Memorial Museum, gives a comprehensive introduction to the Holocaust.

http://jewishmuseum.lv
Here you can learn all about Jewish populations in Latvia, both historically and those who live there today.

https://minorityrights.org/country/latvia
Both an overview of minority rights in different countries and an exploration of minority rights in Latvia are included here.

LIFESTYLE

People in Latvia take advantage of fun activities, such as hot-air ballooning.

7

ACROSS THE GLOBE, MANY UNIQUE lifestyles can be found. Some are restrictive; others are open. Some are steeped in tradition, while still others are being remade and reimagined. The Latvian lifestyle mixes the traditional and the contemporary. As residents of a Baltic state, Latvians have retained some of their ancient heritage, such as festivals and foods, while other customs have fallen away. As years pass, new traditions take shape. Familial roles, career expectations, and life experiences evolve. Latvia is a country of varied ethnic groups, ages, genders, and economic classes, among other differences. For that reason, each family's lifestyle will look different. This is the beauty of an independent country that values and supports free will and decision-making.

"A high early male mortality rate means that there are 8 percent more women than men in the country."
—BBC News, 2010

LATVIAN LIFE

The soul of the Latvian is tied to the care of the land and the soil. A Latvian proverb illustrates this feeling perfectly: "He who cares for the land will be fed by the land." This attachment to the soil is evident in much of Latvian tradition, as well as in their literature, painting, music, and sculpture.

A typical Latvian family has one or two children.

The makeup of the extended Latvian family is similar to that in other Western countries—father, mother, children, grandparents, aunts, and uncles— and family ties are usually strong. One to two children is considered the ideal, and kids are usually born and brought up in the family home, where they are taught to assume the roles that they will play later in life.

Since Latvia regained its independence, women have enjoyed the same legal rights as men. Likewise, they have gained recognition and representation in political spheres. In 2018, thirty-one of the one hundred Saeima seats were filled by women. Further gains have been made elsewhere too. As has been the case in many European countries, it is more acceptable in the twenty-first century for women to work outside the home in a variety of jobs. Women have more choice and more autonomy now than ever before.

WOMEN

Women make up of the majority of the population of Latvia. According to 2017 estimates, there are 0.85 males for every female in Latvia. Some news outlets have reported that this makes it difficult for women to find suitable partners. If the Latvian population continues to decrease, there may be more issues like these in the future.

Women are entitled to sixteen weeks of paid maternity leave. They can extend that for another eighteen months of unpaid parental leave and still hold on to their jobs. Life expectancy for women is longer than for men. In 2017, life expectancy was 79.5 years for females and 70.1 years for males.

Politically, women are gaining more footholds as well. As of 2018, women made up nearly a third of the Saeima. Latvia had its first female prime minister in 2013, though she resigned after two years in office.

In the fashion industry, per capita, Latvia produces more female models than most other countries in the world. Some popular models from Latvia include Ginta Lapina and Inguna Butane.

Several people affected Latvian perceptions of women dramatically. Prominent among them is former president Vaira Vike-Freiberga. Sandra Kalniete, whose credentials include art historian and author, was Latvia's EU commissioner (2004), ambassador to the UN (1993–1997), party leader of Civic Union, and elected member of the European Parliament (2009). Marie N (Marija Naumova) is a popular singer who won the Eurovision Song Competition in 2002. Agnese Koklaca is an Olympic luger who finished twenty-fourth at the 2010 Olympics. Daina Taimina is a well-known Latvian mathematician who teaches at Cornell University, specializing in crocheted objects. Her book *Crocheting Adventures with Hyperbolic Planes* won the 2012 Euler Book Prize. Laila Pakalnina is a screenwriter and film director who has directed more than twenty films since 1991. Her latest film, *Ausma*, was released in 2015.

Agnese Koklaca trains in the luge for the 2010 Olympics.

Latvia is not a cheap place to live, but its largest city, Riga, is more affordable than other European cities. When compared to places like Paris, London, and Barcelona, Latvia offers similar sophistication at a much lower price. Apartments, entertainment, and food can all be had at affordable prices compared to Western European cities.

ELDERS

A popular Latvian proverb states, *Ka vecie svilpo ta jaunie danco*. Its translation is, "The young ones dance as the old ones whistle." Older people have an important role in passing on traditions to the next generation because they are usually the guardians of customs and beliefs and the holders of knowledge and wisdom. Unfortunately, many elderly people live below the poverty line. During the transition period after regaining independence, the Latvian government was unable to improve this situation by increasing pensions. The average old-age pension in 1995 was only about 35 percent of the average wage. As a result, elderly people often become dependent on their children to maintain their standard of living. Approximately 20 percent of the population of Latvia is sixty-five years or over (2017 estimate).

PROPERTY

The rural share of the population declined from 34 percent in 2005 to 32 percent in 2016. Young people flock to the cities for better-paying jobs, an improved living environment, and access to various services. For decades, the majority of Latvians in urban areas lived in below-standard housing, due to the construction and ownership of all accommodations by the state during Soviet rule. The apartments built during this period were of very poor quality and received limited maintenance over the fifty-year period. Apartments had only one or two rooms, a small kitchen, and a bathroom that was often shared with other families. They were known as Khrushchyovka. They were often concrete-paneled or made of brick. Though many of these buildings have been demolished, others are still in use today. About 68 percent of Riga's residents live in micro-districts made up of these apartment buildings that have long surpassed their fifty-year life expectancy.

Apartment buildings are a popular choice for young people. This one is in Riga.

With the regaining of independence and the reinstatement of private ownership of property, there is extensive renovation being carried out on older private homes, apartments, farms, and public buildings, as well as the construction of new ones. Some people own their apartments, which they have been able to buy in new, privately owned buildings. It has been a challenge to institute organized housing programs or co-op housing structures, as Latvians are generally suspicious of anything that reminds them of the housing policies of the Soviet era. Riga and some of Latvia's coastal cities are home to new buildings that house luxury apartments and penthouses owned by vacationers.

FARMS

During the Soviet period, the urban garden was often a necessity to supplement the meager food supplies with basics such as potatoes, onions, and cabbage, and it continues to play the same role to some extent. However, spiritually, the garden is to the city dweller what the cottage is to the North American—a place to relax, to sit in the sun, and to get out of close living quarters in the city.

In the countryside, the collective farm system that existed during the Soviet era has disappeared. All farms are now held privately. After Latvia joined the EU and additional funding became available, most farms became modernized, increasing productivity, and many have taken steps to become all-organic farms. The organic sector looks to become an increasingly prosperous export for Latvian farmers. Domestic sales are also up, as more and more Latvians are turning to healthy, locally sourced, all-natural diets. The farming sector focuses primarily on grain, potatoes, fruits, berries, milk, pork, poultry, and veal.

BIRTH

Latvia's mortality rate for newborn babies is close to 5.2 per 1,000 births (2017), significantly lower than it had been twenty years earlier. Studies of the Baltic region link higher infant mortality rates in Latvia (as compared to Lithuania and Estonia) to less successful adjustment to new health, economic, and political situations following the fall of the Soviet Union.

FAMILIES

For a Latvian family, the arrival of a newborn child is a time for much celebration. Parents usually appoint relatives as godparents, in the belief that children inherit their godparents' good qualities. A baby girl may have two godmothers and one godfather, and a baby boy may have two godfathers and one godmother. Traditionally the baby's name is announced during a formal ceremony (called Krustaba) in which the godparents promise to care for the child in the event that the parents cannot. The newly named child is then introduced to the guests and welcomed as a full-fledged member of the family.

WEDDINGS

Another major event is the wedding, which usually begins with a formal proposal of marriage. A century or more ago, this was done through intermediaries speaking to the mother of the bride-to-be and then to her father and brothers.

Latvians have many unique wedding traditions. One of the most beloved is the "gates of honor." In this ritual that occurs on the wedding day, the bride and groom must pass through a "gate" erected by wedding guests—both invited and uninvited! The guests make a large gate of honor by holding boughs of leaves and plants. It is said that the larger the gate, the more prosperous and positive the marriage will be.

Weddings are a joyful and ceremonial occasion.

Once the proposal was accepted, a party was held at the bride's house, which often lasted right through the night. Nowadays, the bride and the groom decide how their wedding will be celebrated.

Today, the modern wedding ceremony often takes place in a church, where the bride gets married wearing traditional white and attended by bridesmaids. However, before that, the bride and groom have most likely already seen each other. Traditional wedding customs often find the groom entering the bride's preparation location, only able to see her after he passes a series of tests given to him by a "witch." To lead them into church and to host celebrations afterward, the bride and groom often invite another couple (*vedeji*), usually older than them. Some wedding celebrations last for three days—even lasting for over a week in some cases! Another curious tradition is that the bride often wears her veil until midnight of the wedding night. At that point, she gives the veil to her sister or another female relative, encouraging a succession of marriage.

The singing of special songs is an important part of the wedding ritual. After the church ceremonies, a feast is held during which the newlyweds are initiated as married people. The bride's coronet is replaced with a headdress commonly worn by married women, and the bridegroom is offered a hat appropriate for married men. A shawl is then placed over the shoulders of the couple, and the guests sing them a song welcoming them to married life.

PUBLIC HEALTH

The recent long years spent under Soviet dominance have resulted in poor living conditions in Latvia and the neglect of health. The birthrate is low (9.7 births per 1,000 population), and the death rate is the fourth-highest in the world (14.5 deaths per 1,000 population). Overall life expectancy is 74.7 years.

Latvia's health-care system is universal, state-funded through taxation. The state pays for most benefits. According to a 2016 report by the Organization for Economic Co-operation and Development (OECD), Latvia's system, for the most part, delivers effective and efficient care. Over the past few years, Latvia has strengthened its primary care and consolidated its hospitals, increasing efficiency and access.

Challenges noted by the OECD include long waiting times for test results, as well as high copayments for many medical procedures, which leaves many Latvians foregoing treatment because they cannot afford the cost. One in seven Latvians report that they have gone without health care due to the cost, distance, or waiting times. When counting only low-income individuals, the number increases to one in three Latvians. Additionally, the health system has not prioritized data systems to measure, compare, and improve care.

A related concern in the country is the continued rise of smoking and alcohol consumption, which continue to become more common, contributing to health issues across the population.

Latvia's health-care system is still growing and overcoming challenges.

SCHOOLS

Many Latvians begin their education at five years of age. The compulsory (basic) education lasts nine years, and preschool attendance for five- and six-year-olds is mandatory. About 99 percent of Latvian people age fifteen and over are able to read and write.

The first law establishing compulsory education for all children was passed in 1919. The language of instruction was the language spoken in the family. The compulsory foreign language was at first German, although it was later replaced by English.

The state finances ethnic minority schools, where courses are taught in Belarusian, Estonian, Hebrew, Lithuanian, Polish, Roma, Russian, and Ukrainian. However, new language reforms were passed in 2018. By September 2021, all sixteen to eighteen year olds will be taught in Latvian. Even in minority schools, 80 percent of classes will be taught in Latvian, a 40 percent increase from past standards. According to lawmakers, the country is passing these reforms in order to raise test scores across the board. Currently, all but one of the lowest-scoring schools is Russian or bilingual. Latvian officials hope to reverse this trend by expanding Latvian education across the country. However,

some ethnic Russians and leaders in Russia see the changes as an oppressive force against the Russian minority in Latvia. They argue that the reforms are a type of forced assimilation.

Latvia places a high priority on education. Education up to secondary school is free, and scholarships are offered for higher education. Latvia had fifty-eight colleges and institutions of higher education in 2018, most of which belonged to the state; the rest were founded by legal entities or private individuals. In 2015, 40 percent of twenty-five- to thirty-four-year-olds in Latvia had completed post-secondary education. Currently, the government is hoping to increase interest in science, technology, engineering, and math (STEM) fields. Schools are offering more courses and instruction in these subjects.

SOVIET SCHOOLING

After World War II, during the period of Soviet occupation, the Latvian school system was changed to reflect Soviet standards, and the curriculum was changed according to socialist political theories. The teaching of Latvia's language and history diminished, and the number of Russian schools increased. Riga Medical Institute was established in 1950, and the Civil Aviation Engineering Institute was founded in 1960.

After regaining its independence, Latvia undid many of the changes imposed during the Soviet period. Latvian history and literature are taught without "political revisions," and Latvian has become the main language of instruction.

The teaching process was also changed with the regaining of independence, moving away from central control of all subjects that were taught to more autonomy within each school. Within guidelines established by the state, schools may vary their curriculum and choose their own teaching methods. The students are taught and encouraged to seek greater personal initiative, independence, and responsibility.

Latvia continues to be a country in transition. It has not fully emerged from its Soviet past, and its health and education systems have not quite smoothed out all the bumps that come from starting anew. As the country strives for progress and achievement, both lawmakers and voters will need to make difficult decisions about what they want their young country to look like.

INTERNET LINKS

http://www.aic.lv/portal/en/izglitiba-latvija
This is the one-stop shop for all things education in Latvia.

http://www.studyinlatvia.eu/en/home
Visit this site for information about higher education in Latvia, especially for students considering studying abroad for college or graduate school.

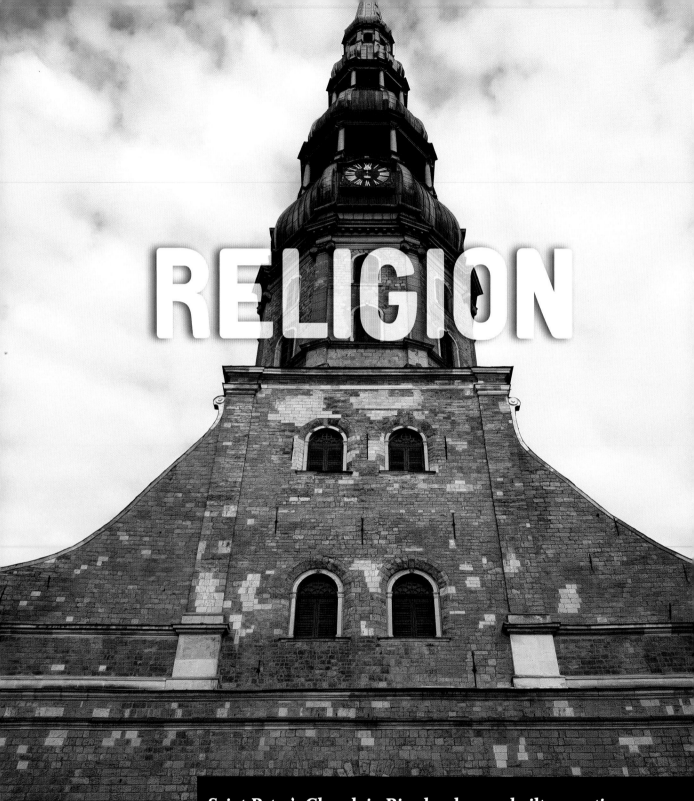

RELIGION

Saint Peter's Church in Riga has been rebuilt many times.

LIKE MANY PARTS OF LIFE IN LATVIA, religion there is steeped in old traditions and ancient practices, while also influenced by new organizations and contemporary beliefs. Religious life in Latvia has undergone many transformations. Until World War II, there was a sizeable Jewish population within the country. Most were killed or forced to flee during the Holocaust. During the Soviet years, religion was outlawed. Today, Christian churches are many, but church attendance is low. These many evolutions have developed a Latvia that is a diverse, open, fascinating place to live and visit when it comes to spirituality and religion.

ANCIENT RELIGIONS

Worshippers of Latvia's ancient religions gathered at traditional places such as "holy" hills and lakes, as well as groves of oak or linden trees. All of creation was viewed as a harmonious entity, to be respected and

These people celebrate the midsummer festival, which is a cherished tradition that uses many ancient religious themes.

honored. There were some five thousand original gods, but only three were worshipped as divine beings—Dievs, Mara, and Laima. Worship of these deities goes back a long way. Over time, these old beliefs have been mixed with Christian beliefs. The original traditions are not always obvious, but there is extensive use of the symbols as design elements in textiles, metals, pottery, and wood. Latvians no longer practice the ancient religion, but the tradition lives on in folk songs, legends, and festivals.

THE CHURCH

Christianity was introduced to Latvia in the early 1200s by Eastern Orthodox and Roman Catholic monks and crusaders of the Teutonic Order. Originally, services were held in Latin, and so they were not understood by the Latvians, causing the new religion to spread slowly. It was accepted on the surface, but the familiar traditions and ways held for centuries were continued in secret. Latvians' adherence to their own religious ways was tied closely to the need for continuing resistance against the conquering foreigners.

THE CATHOLIC FAITH

The spread of Christianity was tied to the strengthening of German rule in Livonia and the creation of the dominating ruling classes.

The Catholic faith was introduced into Latvia in 1186 when Meinhard, a German monk, became the first bishop. He built a wooden church to begin his missionary work, but he met with almost no success at first. His successor, Berthold of Hanover, was appointed bishop of Livonia, but he was killed in battle soon after he arrived in 1198.

It was not until the arrival of Bishop Albert of Buxhoeveden, who succeeded Berthold as bishop, nearly twenty years after Meinhard arrived, that the real conversion of the Latvians to Christianity began. This may have been in part due to his entourage of twenty-three ships of armed crusaders. Albert also

HISTORIC RELIGIOUS ARCHITECTURE

Among the best-known and finest examples of Latvian church architecture is the Riga Cathedral, known as Rigas Doms. Started in 1211 by the Germanic bishop Albert I, the original building was in the Romanesque style with round arches, many of which survive to this day. It was added to in the Gothic style during the next two centuries—the pointed arches built next to the round ones and new structures, such as side chapels and a west transept,

were constructed. In the eighteenth century more additions were made in the Baroque style, and in the twentieth century a new entrance hall was built. The cathedral also contains magnificent stained-glass windows depicting themes from the Bible and the history of Riga. Today, services are held each weekday morning, as well as on Sundays. Additionally, the church serves as one of the busiest music venues in Riga.

secured an alliance with King Valdemar of Denmark, who landed in Tallinn, Estonia, with an army in 1219.

The Jesuits attempted to continue the spread of Catholicism after the bishopric ceased to exist in 1563, but with the spread of the Reformation into Latvia soon after, the Catholic Church quickly lost its influence over most of Latvia, except in the eastern Latgale region.

REFORMING CHRISTIANITY

The Protestant Reformation started in Riga in 1521 and soon spread throughout Livonia. Lutheranism—the movement adhering to the doctrine of Martin Luther, the leader of the Protestant Reformation in Germany—in particular was further consolidated under seventeenth-century Swedish domination. The clergy wielded comprehensive influence and power over all aspects of daily life, particularly during the feudal period. Permission was necessary for all important acts of one's life, such as the choice of a husband or wife, the

Saint Peter's is a prominent Lutheran church in Riga.

date for the marriage, the choice of names for children at baptism, or even permission to attend school.

SEPARATION OF CHURCH AND STATE

By the time the Republic of Latvia was established in 1918, there were three principal Christian denominations in the country—Lutheran, Roman Catholic, and Russian Orthodox.

The church was separated from the state, and offenses against an individual's beliefs were forbidden by law. During the years of Soviet occupation, religious freedom for all faiths was suppressed. There was large-scale deportation of clergy, and church property was seized by the state. Some churches were turned into concert halls, museums, warehouses, movie theaters, and meeting halls, while others were burned or left to ruin. Membership in all congregations fell dramatically, although the Catholic Church lost fewer members than the Lutherans.

With the regaining of independence in 1991, religious life returned. Today, Latvia has religious freedom, and the rights of religious organizations are guaranteed by law. Congregations have regained the use of their former properties, and some churches are being restored, though church attendance has not recovered.

AFFILIATION

As in many other nations, while Latvia has a high percentage of people who identify as Christian, only a small percentage attends church regularly. In Latvia, about 7 percent of the population are regular churchgoers. Though church may not be a huge part of daily (or even weekly) life in Latvia, it is certainly a strong part of the country's history. Many still participate in church ceremonies such as weddings and funerals. Each year, the Roman Catholic Church conducts about nine hundred weddings and four thousand funerals, as well as around two thousand First Communions across the country. The Catholic Church is popular with Polish minorities, while Lutheranism continues to be a popular choice for affiliation for others, due in part to historical ties with Nordic countries and Germany. The Lutheran Church dominates in central and western Latvia, while Catholicism is most popular in eastern Latvia. Many ethnic Russians continue to practice Russian Orthodoxy. There are also small numbers of Buddhists, Jehovah's Witnesses, Christian Scientists, Mormons, Muslims, and Jews, among others.

It is important to note that the Latvian census does not seek data on religious or spiritual life. All data comes from reporting by religious organizations themselves, which means that there are large margins for error, and the data can vary greatly depending on the source. A growing percentage of Latvians claim to follow no religion whatsoever. Some historians blame this on the Soviet occupation, which outlawed religious practice. As church attendance decreased and even stopped altogether, religion was not passed down to new generations.

This synagogue in Ventspils shines on a sunny day.

INTERNET LINKS

http://katolis.lv/en/church-in-latvia.html
The official page of the Catholic Church in Latvia offers information, history, scriptures, and contacts.

http://www.latvia.travel/en/sight/riga-st-peters-church
Learn all about this beautiful, tall, historic church located in Riga.

https://www.mormonnewsroom.org/facts-and-statistics/country/latvia
The Church of Jesus Christ of Latter-Day Saints has about 1,200 members in Latvia. Here, you can learn about their mission, beliefs, and growth within the country.

LANGUAGE

In order to accommodate tourists and residents, signs in Latvia offer multiple languages.

9

THE OFFICIAL LANGUAGE OF LATVIA is Latvian, though members of parliament have tried unsuccessfully to have Russian approved as a co-official language. Latvian is used at home, at school, and in the workplace, though other languages may be used in government meetings if everyone agrees. Most newspapers, broadcasts, films, and Latvian web pages are produced in Latvian, though some are also written in Russian, English, and Swedish.

The Latvian language comes from an ancient Indo-European language family that was spoken at about the same time as ancient Greek, Latin, and Sanskrit. Over the centuries, it has been influenced by other languages with which the ancient Latvians came into contact, such as Livonian. Sadly, the last living Livonian speaker passed away in 2013, and the language is now considered "dormant." The Latvian language was also influenced by Old Russian, which added words related to the church and the law courts.

Two men, Juris Alunans (1832—1864) and Atis Kronvalds (1837—1875), made the greatest contributions to the development of a standard Latvian language and uniting literary language and the spoken idioms of the Latvian dialects. Standard Latvian is the official language of Latvia.

Latvian, the official language of Latvia, is heavily influenced by German, but it is most closely related to Lithuanian. Lithuania is located on the southern border of Latvia.

LATVIAN'S HISTORY

In contrast to the language of neighboring Lithuania, Latvian has undergone extensive changes over the last few centuries. The largest addition to the Latvian vocabulary came during the Middle Ages from Middle Low German, which added words in the fields of crafts, fashion, and agriculture. Some very archaic words—for example, *asins* (an original Indo-European word for "blood")—have been preserved. Through trade, wars, and invasions, Latvian has been exposed to the influence of many other languages and cultures, including Finnish, Polish, French, English, and Russian.

Until the nineteenth century, the development of Latvia's language and literature was mainly in the hands of German clergymen. Many of them learned and understood the Latvian peasant language and attempted to keep the influence of their native German on Latvian writing to a reasonable level. As a result, no real separation ever developed between the literary language and popular speech.

The most significant period of development for modern Latvian as it is spoken and written today started early in the twentieth century, when the country was independent for the first time. During those years, Latvian became the principal language of Latvia. During the long period of occupation after the first bout of independence, both Latvian and Russian were considered official languages, but the use of Latvian was discouraged. This changed again after 1990, when Latvia became its own independent country once more.

WRITING AND SPEAKING

The nineteenth century was an important period for the development of both the Latvian written and spoken language. It saw the rise of Latvian national literature, which was the first conscious effort of the Latvians themselves to care for their language. Words were coined for the new notions of Western civilization, a necessary process when a peasant idiom was developing into a cultural language.

The development of Latvian was further strengthened through new literary works—especially those of Janis Plieksans, working under the pen name Rainis, who used his numerous translations of Western European classics to help create new means of expression for his poetry, using words that eventually became part of the language.

Rainis's works were famous for their assertion of national freedom and social consciousness. He was arrested and sent to eastern Russia from Latvia in 1897 because of his socialist political activities, but he returned in 1903 to take part in the unsuccessful revolution of 1905. He then left for Switzerland and did not return again until 1920, after Latvia's first independence had been secured. On his return, he was elected to the Saeima as the minister of education and director of the National Theater.

Rainis translated many international literary works, including Goethe's *Faust* and works by Schiller, Shakespeare, Heine, and Pushkin. These translations extended the Latvian vocabulary and also introduced the usage of shorter word forms. His original works were inspired by historical and international themes. A masterpiece, *Joseph and His Brothers*, is based on a theme of prophecy and forgiveness that appears in the Christian Old Testament and Jewish Talmud.

Today, Latvians address people in multiple ways, according to context, familiarity, and formality. Many people who visit or move to Latvia find themselves adopting new variants of their names in many situations. For instance, William becomes Vil, Vilu, or Vils. Interestingly, many male names in Latvia contain "s" at the end—such as Roberts, Aleksanders, and Oskars. The most popular names in the country are Janis for a man and Anna for a woman.

Rainis was a poet, playwright, and translator.

MODERNITY

After the country gained independence in 1918, new needs arose for its development into a republic with its own identity. Latvian terminology needed to be developed for the law courts, the administrative system, and for the newly established university, art academy, and music conservatory. Official Latvian place names were also needed to replace the old czarist Russian ones.

Present-day standard written Latvian uses a thirty-three-letter alphabet, based on Latin origins. Modern Latvian is expressive and versatile, and is suited for poetry and literature as well as for sophisticated scientific texts.

Presently approximately 56 percent of Latvia's people are native speakers of Latvian, and it is spoken by approximately 1.1 million people. Meanwhile, Russian continues to be commonly heard on the streets of Riga. Latvian is spoken as a first language by minority populations in other European Union countries, Russia, the United States, Canada, Australia, and South America.

THE MEDIA

The media plays an important role in affecting the tone and usage of the two main languages in Latvia—Latvian and Russian. Newspaper circulation figures are fairly small, and the readerships are concentrated around the main cities.

There are six national newspapers, two of which are published in Russian. *Diena*, a national daily published six days a week in Latvian, has a circulation of about thirty-one thousand. Comparatively, Russian newspapers have a much lower circulation. Latvia has one main tabloid, *Vakara Zinas*, and many regional newspapers. In 2008, the National Library of Latvia introduced a digitized collection of historical periodicals. The collection is freely available online and covers the years 1800 through 2000.

DEVELOPING GRAMMAR

The earliest texts in Latvian appeared in the sixteenth century, and the first grammar was developed two centuries later. Janis Endzelins, the most noted Latvian philologist, laid the foundation of modern Latvian grammar and vocabulary through his research and the publication of the book *Latvian Grammar*, which created new words and clarified others.

Present-day written Latvian uses a macron, a mark placed over vowels to indicate vowel length, and an accent over or under a consonant to indicate the softer pronunciation of a letter. (These marks do not appear in this book, however.) There are multiple Latvian dialect groups, and much debate remains over what they should be called. There is a long-standing tradition of dividing them between Low Latvian and High Latvian. These dialect groups are also associated with the West and Central (Low) and East (High). East, or High,

Latvian is also known as Latgalian. Modern-day Latvian is based in West/Central (Low) Latvian.

RADIO, TELEVISION, AND THE INTERNET

Some sixty-nine national, Riga, local, or regional radio stations and two state-funded TV stations broadcast regularly in Latvian and/or Russian. Public Latvian Radio broadcasts in Latvian and Russian, with newscasts in German and English, as well as in the languages of Latvia's ethnic minorities. A total of 81 percent of the population listens to radio at least once a week. Russian state radio is received in Latvia, as are programs from the Voice of America and Radio Free Europe.

Radio remains a popular source for information and entertainment. Latvijas Radio is a popular station in the country.

Latvian state television was established in 1954. An independent channel was established in 1992, with nightly news broadcasts in Latvian and English. Russian state television and a private channel from Moscow also broadcast in Latvia. Cable and satellite television brings in many international broadcasts. News programs, international sporting events such as the Olympics and FIFA World Cup, and quiz shows are all popular television programs in Latvia.

Today, nearly all Latvians have access to the internet. While international social media networks such as Facebook are popular, Latvia's own social network, Draugiem.lv, has a high number of active users. Inbox.lv is one of the most-visited sites in Latvia, as it is a one-stop shop for email, photo, and dating services. In 2016, Netflix expanded its video streaming service to customers in Latvia.

INTERNET LINKS

https://www.baltictimes.com
This site shares the news of Latvia, Estonia, and Lithuania

https://www.leta.lv/eng
Most of Latvia's national news stories are covered here.

Colorful murals are just one example of Latvia's bustling arts community.

10

LATVIA HAD A RICH CULURAL HISTORY long before it became an arm of the USSR, and it continues to center on literature, music, and performing arts as bedrocks of its daily life. Latvian families place a high value on folktales, folk music, and other historical creations. The arts thrive through drama groups, choirs, ensembles, orchestras, and dance groups. Latvians are immensely proud of their heritage and, especially since independence in 1991, strive to express themselves and their identity through prose, plays, and music.

Latvia is famous for its song festivals, which have been in existence since the 1870s. They are popular events in Latvia, as well as in Latvian immigrant communities throughout the world. Several thousand singers take part in the festivals.

Every few years, local towns and districts hold competitions for choirs, orchestras, and dance groups to select the best for a national festival.

"To the Latvians the *dainas* are more than a literary tradition. They are the very embodiment of his cultural heritage."
—Vaira Vike-Freiberga, former president of Latvia

BOOKS

Although Latvian culture is ancient, its literature is relatively new, having only come into its own during the first National Awakening of 1850 to 1880. Before this time, nearly all writing about Latvia was done by foreigners, mainly Baltic Germans.

In 1878 the first classic novel in Latvian, *Mernieku laiki*, was published. It was a comic satire of country life, filled with caricatures of stereotypical Latvians, such as the devout hypocrite, the old gossiper, and others, written by two brothers, Reinis and Matiss Kaudzitis. They spent twenty years writing it. In 1888, the national epic "Lacplesis" (Bearslayer), written by Andrejs Pumpurs and based on Latvian folklore, was published. In 1890, a new era in Latvian literature called the Jaunastrava (New Current) began, in which contemporary problems were depicted through the imagery of folk poetry. The most prominent writer of this period was Janis Plieksans (1865—1929) who used the pen name Rainis. He was born into a well-to-do family. However, he edited a socialist newspaper, and for his activities in the political underground he was arrested, imprisoned, and then banished from Latvia for twenty years. Rainis's wife, who wrote under the name Aspazija (1868—1943), was a well-known author in the 1890s of numerous blockbuster plays with radical feminist themes. In her day, she was recognized as the leading writer of modern Latvian literature. Between them, they laid the foundation for modern Latvian drama, journalism, and literature. Rudolfs Blaumanis (1863—1908) is perhaps Latvia's greatest playwright. He influenced young Latvian writers and authors to raise standards in the nation's language and writing style. Although he is best known for his tragedies, he wrote comedies as well. His characters are set in an everyday environment, and their powerful conflicts related to alcoholism, love and money, and general change form the plot of his plays.

Karlis Skalbe (1879—1945), who was known as the Latvian Hans Christian Andersen, wrote rich nationalistic verses and fairy tales. He was the youngest of ten children and grew up in poverty. Like Rainis, he lived in exile for his anti-czarist activities, and he was one of the first intellectuals to openly discuss the idea of full independence for Latvia.

After Latvia gained independence in 1918, a new period in Latvian literature and drama began, as the literary climate was stimulating, intellectual, and creative. Realism continued to be popular in literature, as were themes that glorified the past, although love themes also became quite popular. Short stories gained popularity in the early 1920s. New newspapers and magazines appeared.

The best-known author of this period—and also considered Latvia's greatest modern poet—is Aleksandrs Caks. He disregarded rhyme and used daring and unexpected images. Although his choice of topics was considered shocking at the time, his poems of the 1930s stand out as remarkable works of art.

This period ended with the occupation of Latvia by the Soviets in the 1940s. Under the Soviet occupation, the sole aim of Latvian literature was to praise communism and Stalinism, so literary work became dull and mainly took the form of industrial and agricultural narratives. Nevertheless, after censorship was relaxed somewhat in the late 1950s, a number of well-known Latvian writers were able to practice their craft throughout the years of Soviet occupation, even though some of them suffered greatly from persecution. Some of the better known include the novelist Alberts Bels and poet Vizma Belsevica. In the 1980s and 1990s, literature in Latvia was no longer subjected to political censorship. Readers had free access to works written in exile by authors such as Astride Ivaska, Roberts Muks, Andrejs Eglitis, and Margita Gutmane. The works of authors and poets such as Knuts Skujenieks (*Seed in the Snow*) and Bronislava Martuzeva (*Roadside Crosses*), who had been deported or imprisoned during the Soviet era, were published.

Literature in the twenty-first century has branched out into various genres for readers of the independence years. Realistic narratives, fiction, and documentary literature that depict memories of deportation or tragic fates of families in the occupation years have had popularity in previous decades. Sandra Kalniete's *With Dance Shoes in Siberian Snows* has been translated into nine languages. The trilogy *Bille* by Vizma Belsevica recounts memories of childhood in the 1930s and 1940s. In 2017, American author Inara Verzemnieks's book *Among the Living and the Dead: A Tale of Exile and Homecoming on the War Roads of Europe* became exceedingly popular both in and out of Latvia. Verzemnieks's memoir recounts her grandmother's stories about the family

Despite long years of foreign dominance and the inevitable erosion of cultural identity, Latvia's vibrancy in the arts is undeniable. Many Latvians use the performing arts as a means to express themselves and the Latvian identity. Song festivals are popular, as are dramas and music. An important part of their musical tradition is folk songs.

Janis Jonevs's first novel, *Jelgava 94*, was a bestseller.

farm left behind in Latvia during World War II. *Jelgava 94* by Janis Jonevs was published in 2013. After winning the European Union Prize for Literature in 2014, the story was being made into a popular film in 2019.

In 2002, a national literature platform was founded in order to preserve the books, plays, stories, and poems that have been produced by Latvians. The center also works to promote Latvian literature on the international stage. The organization promotes events in which Latvian authors and illustrators are featured, such as literature festivals, readings, and workshops. As part of the 2018 centenary celebrations, the Baltic countries were chosen as the Market Focus at the London Book Fair. A hashtag campaign was launched, and reports have been issued in order to promote Latvian authors, illustrators, and booksellers.

CREATIVE PEOPLE

After Stalin's death in 1953, there was a small revival of pre-Soviet Latvian culture, such as folk songs and folktales, and some literary works of past writers were legalized again. Some of the Latvian writers who had been deported to Siberia were also allowed to return to Latvia and write again.

At the end of the Soviet occupation, the poet Mara Zalite turned the classic Latvian epic "Lacplesis" into a rock opera in which the national hero exemplifies nonviolent political action, and the prose of Regina Ezers began to deal with the topic of sensitive individuals isolated and destroyed by a totalitarian environment. Vizma Belsevica, a contemporary novelist, was even considered for the Nobel Prize for Literature in 1992.

In Latvia, directors and actors are held in extremely high regard, almost as if they are Hollywood celebrities. Some of today's biggest names include Karlis Krumins, Viesturs Meiksans, and Valters Silis. Latvia hosts the ever-popular International Festival of Contemporary Theater Homo Novus biannually, as well as the annual Riga Opera Festival.

A very active literary world has also evolved among the Latvians who fled Latvia at the time of the Soviet takeover and settled in various parts of the Western world. Some of the famous names include the essayist and novelist Zenta Maurina, who settled in Germany and later became well known there among the Latvians. Moreover, a whole new generation of Latvian poets also developed in exile in New York and are referred to as the "Hell's Kitchen" school of poets.

The poet Andrejs Eglitis lived in Sweden during the decades after World War II, returning to live in Latvia shortly before his death. He is well known for his patriotic poetry, which describes the longings for the freedom of Latvia. His poem "God, Thy Earth Is Aflame" has been set to music and is considered an important reflection on Latvia's struggle for survival and freedom.

Uldis Berzins is a Latvian poet and translator who has earned many awards and honors. He translates poetry, Bible passages, and other texts into nine languages. In 2016, Berzins received the Dzintars Sodums Award for his translation of the Icelandic *Songs of Edda*, an ancient text.

MUSIC IN LATVIA

Music has long been a part of Latvian cultural life in both formal settings, such as opera houses and theaters, and informal ones, such as the family home or local inn. The enormous variety of musical styles reflects the influences on Latvia's culture from other countries. Latvian folk songs, or *dainas*, make up the largest and most important part of the musical culture of the country. Although hundreds of thousands of written dainas exist, there are believed to be more than one million dainas that have never been published or recorded formally. These songs are sung at special occasions, such as weddings, birthdays, and festivals, accompanied by traditional instruments.

In the middle of the nineteenth century, Latvia experienced a national cultural awakening. Noted composers of that era included Andrejs Jurjans and Jazeps Vitols. The Latvian Symphony Orchestra, founded in 1926, is internationally renowned, as is Kremerata Baltica, a string ensemble led by violinist Gidon Kremer.

Members of the Latvian National Ballet perform *Giselle* in 2013.

BALLET AND OPERA

The Latvian National Opera and Ballet Theater (LNOB) was opened in 1919 and became a representative art institution of the country. It received substantial government support, which allowed it to keep admission fees low and attract many ordinary people to attend. Visits to the opera remained a popular activity for Latvians, particularly during times of oppression and unrest under Soviet and German rule.

The activities of the opera company include opera performances, symphonic concerts, and solo concerts by leading musicians. The National Opera has long played an important role in promoting the works of Latvian composers. A number of Latvian operas were composed and performed between 1920 and 1940, and the company continues to program works by Latvians today. Even during the Soviet occupation, the National Opera continued to perform classical Russian and standard Western repertoire.

Since independence in 1991, the National Opera building has received a major facelift, restoring the original facilities to their former grandeur and adding new ones. Latvian National Opera performances continue to attract major guest performers from Europe and elsewhere. The season runs each year from September to June, with over two hundred performances given during that time.

The ballet company of the National Opera began its work in 1919, with the first performance taking place in 1922. From 1922 to 1944, the company produced twenty-eight one-acts and twenty-three longer ballets, with a total number of 1,536 performances. Soloists performed as guest artists in Europe and elsewhere, and the whole company appeared in guest performances in Sweden and Poland. The National Ballet opened a school in 1932. Among its students were Alexander Godunov and Mikhail Baryshnikov, who was born in Riga, Latvia, to Russian parents. In 1974, he defected to the West while on a performance tour in Canada. Today, Latvia hosts the International Baltic Ballet Festival, which was created by a former principal dancer of the Latvian National Ballet, Lita Beiris.

The opera and ballet companies stage an average of six new productions per company per year. The LNOB also keeps a robust travel schedule, touring to the Luxembourg Opera, the Bolshoi Theatre in Moscow, Russia, and the Hong Kong Festival in recent seasons. In the summertime, the open-air Sigulda Opera Festival is held, featuring an impressive lineup of productions and concerts.

ON STAGE

Professional theater also emerged in Latvia during the National Awakening in the second half of the nineteenth century with the staging of the first Latvian-language production, Schiller's *Die Rauber* (The Robbers), which was directed by Janis Peitans. Adolfs Alunans was the founder of Latvian drama, forming

Though Latvia is small, it has had some popular artists. In 2015, Latvian singer Aminata qualified for the Eurovision Song Contest finals with the song "Love Injected." She won sixth place in the final, which was Latvia's fourth top-ten finish in the history of the contest.

the first Latvian acting company and the early Latvian theater repertoire. The company's first performances took place in Riga in 1868. Latvian professional theater dates from 1886, when the Latvian Society in Riga provided space and funding to support professional actors, laying the foundation for the National Theater of Latvia in Riga, which continues to be one of the foremost theaters in Latvia to this day.

A second theater, Jaunais Rigas Teatris (New Riga Theater), was founded in Latvia in 1902. The reputation of this theater was established with the production of the historical-symbolical plays by Rainis. The set designs were by Janis Kuga, whose scenery and costumes enjoyed wide popularity.

The Daile Theater, founded in 1920, has a capacity of one thousand seats, making it the largest theater in Latvia. It offers regular productions of classic and modern foreign plays, in addition to traditional Latvian dramas. Recent performances have included Latvian translations of *Oedipus Rex*, *Hamlet*, and *A Streetcar Named Desire*.

MUSICAL TRADITIONS

Music as a cultural expression most accurately represents the Latvian character, as it has been very important in the formation and maintenance of national feelings over the centuries. Folk songs are by far the most original and extensive part of Latvian musical tradition.

Latvian folk songs have been passed on from ancient times by direct and verbal communication from one generation to the next. They began to be collected in written form in the nineteenth century, and this continues to the present day. The famous Latvian folklorist Krisjanis Barons spent thirty-seven years classifying the texts of *dainas*, collecting more than 218,000 songs, of which about 35,800 were original.

Latvian folk melodies have influenced the compositions of many Latvian composers of classical music. Pauls Dambis is known for his arrangements of Latvian folk melodies, and Imants Kalnins and Raimonds Pauls are well-known composers. The most famous and prolific Latvian musician is the conductor Mariss Jansons, who conducts many of Europe's best-known orchestras.

SONGS FOR ALL OCCASIONS

The dominant subject of Latvian folk songs is the material and spiritual life of the people. The words deal with the cycle of human life, from cradle to grave, and the songs are arranged this way in the published collections. The first volume contains cradle songs, the second volume love songs, while the third volume has songs about marriage and married life. The fourth volume is on work and everyday life.

A *daina* can be philosophical, humorous, joyful, sarcastic, gentle, instructive, comic, or witty, but actually has very little direct connection with history. Proper names are used to refer only to mythological characters and to those found in the ancient religions. Most dainas are composed of four-line verses that are divided into two—the first two lines ask a question, and the last two give the answer.

Melodies for these songs can be either recitative in style—sung in a group with a lead singer and a responding choir—or solo songs, which are sung solo or in a group. Recitative songs do not have a regular text, as the words are improvised according to the requirements of the subject matter and conditions under which the singing takes place. They are sung to mark the celebration of the seasons or the major events of life—birth, christening, marriage, funerals— or as work songs telling about plowing, threshing, or herding. The solo song texts deal with romance, the beauty of nature, or the sorrows of children and orphans.

CHORAL SINGING

Folk song festivals have become an important part of the Latvian culture. The first nationwide Latvian Song Festival took place in 1873 in Riga to foster and advance choral singing. The choir consisted of several thousand singers (the audience totaled four or five times that number), whereas at the ninth festival in 1938 the chorus consisted of seventeen thousand singers! From the very first song festival, the tradition developed that a nationwide song festival would be held at intervals of four to eight years as an important

Latvians love to sing. It is unusual to find a Latvian who has not sung in a choir or some group at some point in his or her life. For this reason, Latvia is called "the singing nation." Folk songs are one of Latvia's national treasures and date back over a thousand years. The Latvian folk song, or *daina*, is a form of oral art that has the elements of tradition, literature, and symbolism. More than 1.2 million texts and 30,000 melodies have been identified.

Singers at the Latvian Song Festival perform a traditional song.

demonstration of Latvian culture and national unity. In July 2018, the twenty-sixth Song Festival took place in Riga. It marked one hundred years since original Latvian independence. In total, 43,000 people participated, including 18,000 dancers, 16,500 singers, and 8,500 brass players. There were participants from 118 Latvian municipalities and 21 foreign countries.

The program for the Latvian Song Festival has become quite extensive. It may last four to five days or more, and although the main festival takes place in Riga, regional concerts and performances are held throughout Latvia in the weeks before the festival. In addition to the concerts, programs now include arts and crafts exhibitions, folk dance performances, theater, and all kinds of instrumental, vocal, and religious concerts. The 2018 festival featured sixty-five events across twenty-five venues, most of which were free to the public. It took five years and 2,760 people to produce the festival. For the past fifty years, similar song festivals have also been held in many other cities around the world where Latvians have taken refuge.

CRAFTS

Latvia has retained a distinctive folk art, which has its roots in the ancient past but continues to be active and vibrant to this day. Over the centuries, traditional art was evident in buildings and furniture, as well as in the clothes and jewelry that were created for the everyday needs of the rural population. Traditionally, many peasants mastered several crafts and produced their own tools, utensils, and simple pieces of furniture. In addition, each parish had its own craftsmen who specialized in a particular trade.

The fundamental character of Latvian ornamental design is geometric and abstract, and these traditional designs are still applied to contemporary decorative and applied arts, most commonly in ceramics, metalwork, woodwork, textiles, and wickerwork. The creation of applied decorative arts continues to be a dominant and widespread activity in today's cultural life in Latvia.

Fine arts in Latvia found expression from the late nineteenth century. The best-known Latvian painters of that period were Janis Rozentals (1866—1916) and Vilhelms Purvitis (1872—1945).

Latvia may be a small country, but its cultural offerings are large and thriving. Folkways continue to dominate the arts and cultural scenes, but new authors, singers, and artists are appearing every day. If Latvians continue to value their artistic history, there is no limit to the unique creations and performances that will result.

The Riga Christmas Market is full of local handmade gifts.

INTERNET LINKS

http://www.ars-baltica.net/cultural-map/latvia.html
This site offers a "cultural map" of Latvia, including links to film, music, and other performing and visual arts throughout Latvia.

http://latvianliterature.lv/en/news
News, books, writers, grants, and more can be found on the homepage of the nation's literature center.

http://theatre.lv/eng
All the happenings about contemporary performing arts in Latvia can be found here.

LEISURE

Canada (*left*) and Latvia (*right*) battle it out at a pre-Olympic exhibition hockey game in Riga in 2018.

11

EVER SINCE LATVIA GAINED independence, things have been looking up for recreation, as well as relaxation, within the country's forested borders. More and more Latvians are involved in various sports and activities. Increased economic stability has led to more cultural events being offered, such as theater and opera, as well as adventure sports like kayaking. Boating tours and cycling trips have become popular for tourists and natives alike.

Latvians also love to stroll through their city or town parks, taking evening or weekend walks, enjoying some gentle exercise with the whole family. Hockey and basketball are popular sports. Hunting and fishing, hiking, gardening, traditional folk dancing and singing, and craft-making are also popular leisure activities. Latvians can enjoy strolls along the miles and miles of natural, public beaches that line its shorelines. Foraging is also very popular throughout the countryside. Whether they are hunting for mushrooms or berries, Latvians enjoy searching for food in the beautiful, wooded wilderness.

When it comes to Olympic medals, Latvia doesn't have just one standout sport, but the country has produced several winning athletes. Latvians have won gold medals in cycling and gymnastics. Luge, bobsleigh, canoeing, weightlifting, skeleton, and shooting have brought home silver medals.

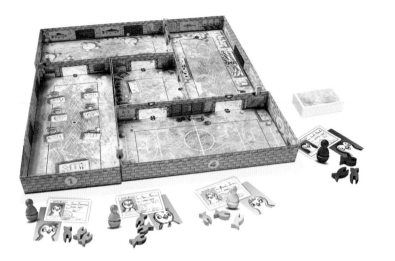

Latvian board game Ice Cool is a fun, winter-themed favorite to play.

GAMES

Games are an integral part of the traditional culture of Latvians. Generally, there are two types—games with music, where the players sing along during the game, and games without music, where participants must perform certain actions.

A traditional game that may be played by children is called *Viens, divi, tris, pedejais paris skiras!* (One, two, three, last couple separate!). Participants form a column, in pairs, except for a single person at the front of the column who does not have a partner. He/she calls out: "*pedejais paris skiras!*" On hearing this, the last couple in the column runs to the front of the column, while the single player tries to catch one of them before they reach the front of the line. Whoever remains single takes over the shouting until a partner is caught again.

Another popular game that is still played in the countryside takes place during Easter. A swing is constructed and hung in the farmyard or nearby woods, and all the inhabitants take a turn on the swing on Easter morning. Gifts are exchanged—particularly colorful Easter eggs—and unmarried men receive hand-knitted mittens or colorful woven sashes from unmarried women, as a token of love.

Contemporary Latvian children don't just play games in their backyards. There are tons of new options for fun, including ice skating rinks, skateboard parks, adventure playgrounds, indoor swimming pools, and more. For young adults, "escape rooms" are a popular group outing, as well as archery centers and drift halls, where adult participants can race on extra-large tricycles.

One enterprising Latvian board game design company made history in 2017. Brain Games, based in Riga, won a prize for Game of the Year in Germany for their "Ice Cool" board game.

STORIES

Despite centuries of foreign dominance, it was through the oral tradition that Latvians developed their culture and identity and preserved their sense of nationality. The most popular activity is singing, but folktales and legends, anecdotes, riddles, proverbs, folk beliefs, and sayings are common too. The usual subject matter is everyday rural life and social customs and behavior.

JOKES AND RIDDLES

Some 450,000 riddles have been collected into the Archives of Latvian Folklore. They are short, usually only two to six words long, and are expressed simply and succinctly. Most have only one correct answer. For example, "What always wears a green frock, summer and winter?" is a spruce tree; "What does not have hands, does not have a loom, yet weaves?" is a spider; "What is high above during the day, down below during the night?" is the sun; and "What flies like a bird but is not a bird, stings like a snake but is not a snake?" is a mosquito. Folk sayings and parables represent collective folk wisdom. Many of the sayings are similar to those of other European cultures because they came into Latvia through the church.

FREEDOM AND TECHNOLOGY

Since the return to independence in Latvia, people have enjoyed a freedom they had not experienced before. The younger generations had never had contact with cultures of the West before the end of Soviet rule. Today, through the popularity of American and European music, movies, and books, leisure activities that were once restricted have broadened. The older generations are relishing a return to their national identities, be they Latvian, Russian, or otherwise.

One of the biggest changes that the twenty-first century has brought to Latvia is the introduction of the internet. In 2017, Latvia had the world's seventeenth-fastest internet speeds. Most homes and public spaces now have

Latvian wrestler Anastasija Grigorjeva (*right*) went to the Olympics for women's wrestling in 2016. Here, she competes against Risako Kawai of Japan during the games.

Wi-Fi. There are also free public Wi-Fi beacons near payphones in Riga. Users can access the beacons when they are within 328 feet (100 meters) of the payphone. As the constitution provides for freedom of speech and freedom of the press, there are no restrictions on browsing or expressing oneself via the internet. In addition to Wi-Fi access, most Latvians now carry cell phones, including smartphones.

SPORTS AND THE OLYMPICS

Sports are popular in Latvia. Soccer, basketball, volleyball, track and field, wrestling, tennis, ice hockey, orienteering, motor sports, or even beach volleyball all take place, weather permitting, around the country.

Swimming is popular with Latvian youngsters, and there are municipal pools in most big towns and cities. In fact, Latvia boasts eighty-one public swimming pools, as well as ninety-two sports schools and clubs. Schools also encourage swimming as part of the physical education curriculum. Latvians also are known for winter sports such as bobsled and hockey. They are usually placed in the top eight for both sports at the Olympics.

Hockey has been the national sport in Latvia since the 1930s, when it first became popular in the country. The first Latvian national hockey team debuted in 1936, but the country didn't have its own artificial ice rink until 1960. Prominent Latvian hockey players include Zemgus Girgensons, who played in an NHL All-Star Game in 2015, and Sandis Ozolins, who was a Stanley Cup champion during his National Hockey League career.

The country also claims a national soccer team. In Latvia, the sport is called "football," but it is the same as soccer in the United States. It was first introduced to Latvia over one hundred years ago by Englishmen who traveled to the country. In 2004, the national team qualified for the EUFA European Championship finals. The most recognizable player on the team is Maris Verpakovskis, who is a top scorer and is very popular.

Latvia is also home to many unique sports, such as BMX biking, beach volleyball, bobsledding, and even mountain skiing. Track events such as javelin are popular, and Latvians have their own Archery Federation that hosts competitions and training sessions.

Latvia's debut in the Olympics took place in 1924, when thirty-eight athletes joined in the summer games. The most famous early Olympian was the long-distance walker Janis Dalins, who won the silver medal for the 31-mile (50 km) walk in 1932. In total, since the 1952 Olympic Games, Latvian athletes have won four gold, fourteen silver, and ten bronze medals. In the 1992 Winter Olympics, Latvia rejoined the Olympic organization as an independent nation. Igors Vihrovs won a gold medal in gymnastics in 2000, and Maris Strombergs won a gold medal in BMX bicycle racing in 2008 and again in 2012. In 2016, Latvia sent thirty-four athletes to Rio de Janeiro, Brazil, to compete in the Summer Olympics. That was also the first year since regaining independence that Latvia failed to win a single medal.

While Latvia may not yet be an athletic powerhouse or global destination for recreational activities, natives and tourists can find much to enjoy. As part of the EU, Latvians can easily find rest and adventure through convenient travel, though many are happy for opportunities within their home country.

INTERNET LINKS

https://www.fifa.com/associations/association=lva/index.html
At FIFA's website, you can learn all about Latvia's national soccer team, their current matches, and their world standings.

https://www.olympic.org/latvia
The homepage of the Latvian Olympic Committee has all the facts and history about the Latvian Olympic Team.

https://worldarchery.org/member/lat/latvian-archery-federation
Learn more about professional archery in Latvia.

FESTIVALS

The midsummer festival is celebrated with traditional outfits, flower wreaths, and dancing.

12

WHEN LATVIA GAINED ITS independence, the state was faced with a new challenge: which traditions and festivities should it keep, and which should it give up in favor of new celebrations? Today, Latvians celebrate a full calendar of holidays and festivals that span the seasons. Some are based in nature, while others commemorate happy and sad days in history.

The festival of Martini takes place in November to mark the onset of winter. There are various festivities in the springtime, celebrating the equinox and the beginning of the summer. The biggest festival of the year, Jani Diena, celebrates the summer solstice and involves singing, dancing, and feasting. Houses are cleaned and foliage is used to make wreaths and garlands.

Traditionally, at the end of the summer, there are two more festivals—one in August to celebrate the end of the hot period and another in September to welcome the fall equinox and remember the souls of the dead.

Due to Latvia's unique history, many festivals celebrated are a combination of ancient and contemporary beliefs. Common features in many festivals are singing and dancing. Christian holidays such as Christmas and Easter are also celebrated and are usually family affairs. Historical holidays commemorating the struggle for independence are also observed.

MIDSUMMER NIGHTS AND DAYS

Many of the festivals combine ancient beliefs with modern celebration, and nowhere is this more apparent than in Latvia's most popular holiday, Jani Diena (Jani's Day). The festival, which celebrates midsummer, begins on the evening of June 23 and continues into the next day. As the festival approaches, songs with a special refrain resound everywhere, awaiting the arrival of Janis (pronounced Yah-niss), an ancient god of new beginnings, who personifies the festival. Generally, Janis is pictured as a tall and handsome man, dressed in beautiful clothes and riding a large horse. He wears the traditional adornment of the occasion—a wreath of oak leaves—on his head. The day before Jani is called Herbal Day because people collect flowers and leaves to make wreathes that will be worn the following day.

On the evening of June 23, called Ligo Vakars or Jani Vakars (Jani's Eve), the celebration of the summer solstice takes place. Jani's Eve has retained most of its ancient pre-Christian flavor. This means a whole night of singing, dancing, merriment, and fortune-telling, until the sun comes up the next morning. Special beer is brewed, and a special cheese is prepared. After dusk, fires are lit on the hilltops. Some brave souls attempt to jump back and forth over them, which is an ancient tradition. The day following the festival is also a public holiday. It is known as St. John's Day.

FLOWERS AND DECORATIONS

June 23 is also considered the best day of the year to gather medicinal herbs. Flowers and greenery are collected to make wreaths of flowers for the women and men—especially men named Janis (the most common men's name)—to wear during the festivities. Everything is decorated with greenery, while mountain ash branches, thistles, and other sharp objects are placed over building entrances to ward off evil spirits.

The following day's activities include old customs believed to enlist the aid of the spirits of the home, field, and forest. They are intended to help provide a good harvest, by shielding crops and livestock from evil.

CHURCH HOLIDAYS

Many Latvian holidays are very similar to those in other Western countries. Latvians celebrate all the main holidays of the Christian world, with the biggest celebrations taking place at Easter and Christmas.

There are echoes in the modern celebrations of ancient festivals that were once observed in Latvia at the same time of year before the coming of Christianity. Christmas and Easter are times for reflection and jubilation for both Christian and non-Christian families. They are special occasions when the whole family can gather together. Latvians always celebrate in style, and everyone makes an effort to dress up for the occasion.

'TIS THE SEASON

Christmas—the Latvian word for the holiday is Ziemassvetki, meaning "winter feast"—not only celebrates the birth of Jesus Christ but also reflects a direct

The winter holidays in Latvia are full of lights, markets, and family time.

connection with the ancient winter solstice celebrations held by Latvians long ago. Pre-Christian Latvian pagan traditions note Christmas as the rebirth of the Sun Maiden, rather than the birth of Jesus. Christmas in Latvia today is a mix of the ancient paganism, contemporary religious beliefs, and ethnic traditions.

Christmas is by far one of the most festive occasions for Latvians—the return of light at the winter solstice is heralded by the arrival of the celestial beings called Dievadeli and the Four Brothers Ziemassvetki, who represent the four days traditionally allowed for celebration of the Christmas period.

Typically at this time, houses are decorated with straw and feathers, and with *puzuri* (PU-zu-ri), diamond-shaped chandelier decorations made from straw or twigs. Tables are set high with generous amounts of different foods, such as pig's snout, gingerbread cookies, bacon rolls, and boiled brown peas.

Many homes and buildings in Latvia also feature decorated trees. By some accounts, Riga is the birthplace of the first Christmas tree, put up in 1510. Today, the trees are decorated with ornaments and candles.

WINTER MASQUERADE

During the weeks before Christmas, the *budulu* custom is celebrated. Disguised in costumes and accompanied by singing, dancing, and much joviality, people call on their friends and neighbors. The festive masqueraders—called mummers—represent good spirits, whose songs and dances are intended to bring good luck to people, fertility to the fields and livestock, and to warn off death. Their dances are characterized by "stomping" steps designed to stomp out all the weeds from the fields. The procession also drags a Yule log along, to be burned at the last stop. This represents the sun recovering its warmth, as well as consuming the past year's misfortunes.

TRADITIONAL ACTIVITIES

Fortune-telling is a popular activity during Christmas and New Year celebrations. Molten lead is poured into water, where it solidifies into an abstract form. The future is predicted by studying the shape of the shadow cast on a wall by this "sculpture." Additional fortune-telling activities include counting the

ANCIENT FESTIVALS STILL REMEMBERED

Many festivals were celebrated in Latvia years ago, marking the changing seasons. Ritual activities took place and special foods were eaten. Today, many of these are still celebrated.

Meteni . . . . *Celebrated in February, the end of* kekatas *(TYEH-kah-tuss)—the carnival activities of Christmas—with sleigh rides and masquerades. Weavers made cloth with their freshly spun yarns, and on the farm young horses were broken in.*

Great Day . . . . *Celebrated on the day and night of equal length—the spring equinox. The ritual activities included washing before sunrise in running water, hanging swings, and chasing birds. It was the time when the days were longer, and the farmers no longer had to use lights in the evenings.*

Usini . . . . *The official beginning of summer, this day was celebrated many centuries ago in April, when roosters were killed in order to silence them, and their blood was drained into horse troughs. Crosses were painted on doors with the blood, and horses were taken to swim before sunrise. The ritual foods were eggs, boiled rooster, and beer. The evening grazing of horses and cattle began, and it was plowing and sowing time for the farmers.*

Jani Diena . . . . *The longest day and shortest night—the summer solstice. The activities were similar to those of today—flower wreaths were made, bonfires were lit, and songs were sung. The ritual foods were cheese, bread, pies, meat dishes, and beer. On the farm, haying started.*

Apjumibas or Rudenaji . . . *The fall equinox and the beginning of the period of the shadows, when the spirits of the dead visit. Lots of meat was eaten and winter crops were sown.*

Martini. . . . . *Celebrated in November, this is the end of the celebration of the souls and the beginning of masquerade time, leading up to Christmas. Martini balls—made of peas, beans, potatoes, and hemp—were the festival food.*

stars to determine how big your harvest will be and peering into the fireplace upside-down and backwards in order to get a glimpse of your future spouse!

Easter, which is a three-day affair in Latvia, traditionally begins with rising early to see the sunrise, washing one's face in an east-running stream, and calling out to the birds. This ensures a healthy, beautiful year. A common tradition on Easter Sunday in Latvia is for neighbors to gather at a swing hung from a pole between two trees and watch as young people try to swing as high as the treetops. Swinging high ensures a good harvest during the coming summer. Gifts are also exchanged, particularly colorful Easter eggs.

Flower crowns and other decorations are sold for the Jani festival every June.

MORE HOLIDAYS

Some of the Latvian holidays also celebrate events that have made deep impressions on Latvia's history and on the lives of its people.

June 14 is the commemoration day of victims of the communist terror when, on the night of June 13, 1941, the first mass deportations were made by the Soviet powers. Some fifteen thousand Latvians from all walks of life, including the old, the sick, children, and even babies, were arrested without trial or legal justification. They were herded into freight trains and transported under guard to Siberia to forced labor camps, or gulags.

November 11, Lacplesis Day, is the memorial day of the fight for independence, commemorating all who have fought in defense of Latvia. The week between November 11 and November 18 is known as Patriot Week. During the week, everyone wears small ribbons in the colors of the nation's flag, in order to send the message, "Latvia is in my heart no matter where I go." November 18 celebrates Latvia's declaration of independence in 1918, and May 4 is the date of the declaration of renewed independence in 1990.

In 2018, Latvia officially marked its centenary: one hundred years of independence. The centenary calendar featured a whole slate of celebrations from 2017 to 2021. To start, one hundred oak trees were ceremonially planted along Latvia's border, laying strength for the next century. A White Tablecloth Celebration marked the anniversary of the Declaration on the Restoration of Independence in 1990. Throughout the five-year period, the centenary was to be marked by programs for children, the twenty-sixth Song and Dance Celebration, a national encyclopedia, special films, and a project highlighting national costumes.

The Latvian calendar is full of a unique mix of holidays and festivals. Some are historical in nature, while others commemorate seasons and help Latvians remember that we are all brothers and sisters on planet Earth. They remember sad days and happy days. And they are sure to take time off! In Latvia, national holidays are taken seriously. The banks close, families get together, everyone dresses up, and a real holiday is had.

Jani's Day, or Jani Diena, is one of the oldest Latvian holidays. However, it isn't just Latvian. The summer solstice is celebrated by people all over the world, though the celebrations often have differing names and traditions. Those in Finland call it Juhannus, while Iranians celebrate Tiregan, and the Dragon Boat Festival is celebrated in East Asia.

INTERNET LINKS

http://www.latvia.eu/history/national-holidays
Check out this infographic of holidays in Latvia that was created by the Latvian government.

http://www.latvia.eu/patriots-week
This website offers an in-depth look at Latvian Patriot Week, a tradition that started in 2007.

https://www.latvia.travel/en/article/summer-solstice-celebrations
This article looks at some of the ways Latvians celebrate the summer solstice each June.

FOOD

Bread—especially rye bread—is a favorite in Latvian kitchens.

F YOU VISIT THE BALTIC COUNTRIES, you'll notice that many of them have similar cuisines. Much of the food is harvested and produced locally. Latvians have been eating their favorite dishes for centuries! Because Latvians often eat local foods, most of the meals in Latvia are in tune with the seasons. Winter, summer, spring, and fall all have their own specific foods and flavors. Food here is hearty—grains, fish, meat, cabbage, and eggs. There is a rich cultural history of preservation, such as salting and canning.

A MUST-HAVE

Bread was—and still is—a staple food at every meal, baked from rye or barley flour, or for special occasions, from wheat or buckwheat flour. Dough for bread was prepared in a large, elongated wooden trough, approximately 4 feet (1.2 m) in length, with handles. The bread was baked in special ovens, where the loaf was placed on a flat, wide wooden shovel to be transferred onto the hot coals.

Baking was done in large quantities, usually in big loaves. On special occasions, rolls might also be baked, with butter and/or egg wash added, or with special toppings, such as grated carrots. Today, Latvians still love their rye bread and eat it with almost every meal. Toast is popular at breakfast.

MEAT AND PORRIDGE

Years ago, porridge was the most commonly served dish and was prepared from pearl barley and other grains. Vegetables, as well as milk, and some meat or lard were added. The content of the porridge or gruel usually depended on what produce was available at a given time of year, or the financial situation of the household.

Oatmeal or barley porridge is still popular, though today it can be found in "instant" versions that simply heat in the microwave! International trade has expanded the availability of fruits, vegetables, and most foods during all months of the year, though some Latvians have returned to strictly local eating in order to be more sustainable, environmentally conscious, and healthy. Organic produce is gaining in popularity across the country.

Meat was traditionally consumed sparingly and on special occasions, since most of it was taken to the market to be sold. Only affluent families could afford to eat meat regularly, and in the countryside fresh meat was often only available when an animal was slaughtered, usually in the fall. Every part of the animal was prepared for consumption—the best cuts were usually sold and the secondary cuts prepared for home consumption, including the blood, head, feet, and innards. Latvian meat dishes may include fowl, beef, pork, and fish. Families who lived along the coasts smoked fishlike eel, flounder, lamprey, and cod. Today, meat or fish is featured in most main dishes. Pork is extremely popular and unofficially known as the "national meat." Pork schnitzel, grilled pork chops, pig ears, and bacon are all favorites.

MORE FLAVORS

Latvian food is traditionally bland and without strong spices. Caraway seeds, onions, and garlic improve the taste. Ground hemp seed prepared with salt

and green onions is sometimes used in place of butter. Fresh milk is added to porridge and gruel, or made into yogurt and cottage cheese. Latvians like to eat honey as a natural sweetener, and honeybees feature prominently in folk songs. Honey production is the business of many farms today.

In terms of side dishes, potatoes and cabbage take center stage. Whether the potatoes are boiled, fried, mashed, or otherwise prepared, they are usually present. Cold salads, pickled items, soups, and boiled peas all make an appearance on family tables.

These bees in Latvia are busy producing honey inside a hive.

JUICES AND OTHER DRINKS

Traditionally, juice prepared from birch or maple sap was a very popular nonalcoholic drink. It was prepared in the springtime in large quantities so that it could last most of the summer.

Today, ale and beer are sometimes made at home. Other popular drinks include juices, soft drinks, and water. Milk is used for drinking, but a Russian ban on milk importation put in place in 2014 is still having effects on Latvia. Prices are down for milk as dairy farmers struggle to adjust, and milk consumption remains stagnant within the country.

MEALTIMES

Latvians usually eat three meals a day. In the olden days, a fourth meal was often added in the afternoon. In those days, the midday meal was usually the main meal of the day—gruel served with lard or fat, and cabbage or sauerkraut. The afternoon extra meal included bread, cottage cheese, buttermilk, and sometimes herring. It helped hardworking farmers stay fueled for the afternoon. Latvians have always been great fans of dairy products. Milk, *ruguspiens* (a sour, carbonated drink, similar to yogurt, with a little bit of alcohol), cottage cheese, cream, cheese, and butter are eaten at almost every meal. Yogurt and cheese sales continue to soar, especially for new and interesting types of cheeses. The year 2007 marked the opening of Milk Manor, a museum all about milk and dairy production in Latvia.

For traditional suppers, Latvians ate potatoes with a flour or mushroom gravy, or milk gruel with bread. Each day of the week, a particular type of dish was served, and dinner on Saturdays as well as the meals on Sundays might also include some special dishes or treats. Today, mealtimes include all sorts of meats, vegetables, and porridges. Latvians love dessert and never hesitate to include a cake, ice cream, or other sweet dish in their meal plans.

ENJOYING FOOD AND DRINK

Latvians are known for their strong hospitality. A guest in anyone's home will always be treated well. Latvians like to entertain, and a formal dinner is taken seriously. Like other inhabitants of the northern countries, Latvians like to eat and drink. They usually have drinks together with a meal.

Dishes prepared for a Latvian feast are chosen according to the produce available at a particular time of year, but the central dish of any festive meal

is the meat course. Food is most plentiful in the fall when the harvest has been brought in—special breads are baked for the occasion. Oven-baked turnips are served, as are carrots, peas, potatoes (cooked and served with fried smoked bacon), onions, and hemp seed, formed into balls. Honey and apples are served for dessert, as well as a rich cake on very special occasions.

One of the main attractions at festivals and fairs is the delicious variety of food.

AUTUMN FEASTS AND FESTIVALS

Traditionally, special family occasions were usually held in the fall when food was plentiful. On special feast days, such as Martini in November, goose or chicken was served. For Christmas and New Year's Eve, traditional dishes included smoked pig's snout, braised sauerkraut or cabbage, and blood pudding served with red bilberry preserves, peas, and beans. For special occasions in the spring, eggs were the favorite dish, as well as jellied veal or pork and milk pudding. For summer festivities, the traditional dishes were made with dairy products, such as cheeses, served with specially baked rolls, butter, and *piragi* (PEE-raa-gi)—crescent-shaped baked buns filled with savory onion and bacon. Riga still holds a city-wide festival each autumn that features crafts, fresh fall treats, and large vats of delicious pumpkin soup.

EATING IN LATVIA TODAY

Latvian cuisine has been influenced by German, Swedish, and Russian cuisine. Today, the foods that Latvians eat are very similar to those eaten in many other countries. Breakfast usually consists of coffee, boiled or fried eggs, fried potatoes, rye or white bread, and butter or cottage cheese. In fact, rye bread is featured in almost every meal. Latvians love this dark, slightly bitter bread!

Lunch may be a hearty soup with meat, and a meat dish followed by a dessert of fruit compote, bread pudding, or a bread soup with raisins or apples.

A Latvian supper may consist of many different dishes, such as milk soup, pasta, porridge with meat, fried fish, boiled potatoes with pork, or cottage cheese. After supper, the typical Latvian may drink milk, tea, or coffee with bread, butter, jam, or honey.

On Sundays, there is usually a more elaborate meal with a special main course, such as meat patties, meat loaf, or cabbage rolls. Desserts such as pancakes with jam or fruit trifle are prepared.

Latvians also enjoy eating out at restaurants. There are a wide variety of restaurants available in Riga, including fast food franchises like McDonald's, KFC, and Hesburger, a popular restaurant chain from Finland that has recently made its way to Latvia. Additionally, Riga is home to many world-class restaurants serving farm-to-table meals, tasting menus, lavish brunches, and so much more.

Whether you are cooking or eating in Latvia, you are taking part in history. Foods here have always been homegrown, preserved, and carefully prepared. Hearty dishes, whether bland and basic on a daily basis or more elaborate during feast days, are commonplace. You'll never feel hungry after a Latvian meal! Meat, grains, fish, and vegetables have always been staples of the diet, and that hasn't changed, even through centuries of political and economic evolution.

INTERNET LINKS

https://theculturetrip.com/europe/latvia/articles/9-latvian-foods -you-must-try-to-eat-like-a-local
This site gives you tips for eating authentically when in Latvia.

http://latvianeats.com
Recipes and stories about traditional Latvian foods are included here.

https://www.lonelyplanet.com/latvia/travel-tips-and-articles/ latvian-cuisine-for-beginners/40625c8c-8a11-5710-a052 -1479d276d764
If you want a basic overview of Latvian food, this page is for you.

CRANBERRY MOUSSE

½ cup farina or cream of wheat
3 cups unsweetened cranberry juice
½ cup sugar
Milk, for serving

Heat juice and sugar in a 2-quart saucepan over medium-high heat. Bring to a boil. Whisk in farina or cream of wheat. Reduce heat to medium-low, and cook, whisking constantly, until thickened. This should take about 5 minutes. Transfer to the bowl of a stand mixer. Put the whisk attachment on the stand mixer. Process on medium-high until thick and doubled in volume, about 12 minutes. If you do not have a stand mixer, whisk by hand until thick. Serve in bowls. Traditionally, a bit of milk is poured over the top.

BEET AND BEAN SALAD

2 cups kidney beans, freshly cooked or from a can
4 medium boiled beets, peeled and cut into cubes
½ cup sour cream
⅓ cup mayonnaise
¼ cup minced gherkins or dill pickles
1 tbsp. kosher salt
Freshly ground black pepper
2 tbsp. sliced parsley leaves

If using canned beans, drain and rinse them. Whisk the mayonnaise, sour cream, and salt together in a large bowl. Stir until smooth. Add beans, pickles, and beets. Stir gently until beans and beets are evenly coated with the mixture. Season with more salt and pepper. Continue stirring. When finished, transfer to a platter. Sprinkle with parsley before serving.

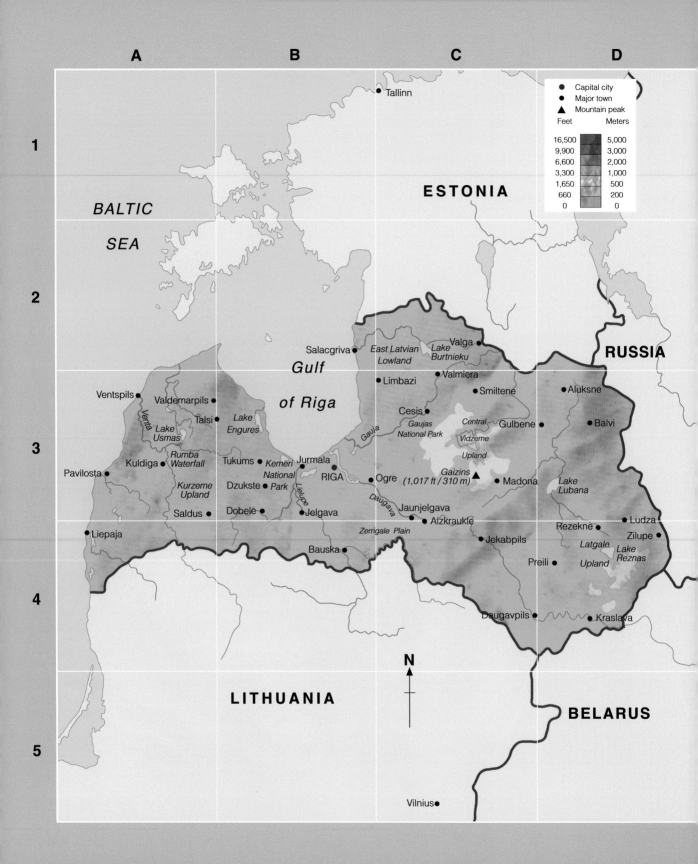

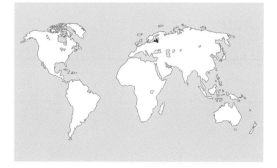

ECONOMIC LATVIA

Agriculture

🌽 Corn

🐔 Livestock

Natural Resources

🪵 Hydroelectricity

🪵 Timber

Manufacturing

🔌 Electronics

🐟 Fish processing

🥫 Food

🪑 Furniture

🏭 Industrial

🛢 Metals

⛵ Ship building

🪵 Textiles

Services

✈ Airport

🚢 Ports

🧍 Tourism

🚂 Train station

ABOUT THE ECONOMY

OVERVIEW

The International Monetary Fund and European Union, along with other donors, assisted Latvia during and after the 2008 global financial crisis. Austerity measures put in place in response to the recession helped the country to bounce back. For a time, the country had high debt and unemployment, though both of those rates have leveled out since 2011. Latvia joined the Eurozone in 2014 and recently installed a progressive tax, which places a slightly higher tax burden on those who have higher rates of personal income, as well as corporations.

GROSS DOMESTIC PRODUCT

$30.32 billion (2017 estimate)

GDP GROWTH

4.5 percent (2017 estimate)

INFLATION RATE

2.6 percent (2017 estimate)

LAND USE

Arable land: 18.6 percent
Permanent pasture: 10.5 percent
Permanent crops: 0.1 percent
Forest: 54.1 percent
Other: 16.7 percent (2011)

CURRENCY

Euro or EUR
US$1 = 0.86 euros (as of 2018)

NATURAL RESOURCES

Peat, limestone, dolomite, amber, hydropower, wood, arable land

AGRICULTURAL PRODUCTS

Cattle, daily foods, grains, potatoes, vegetables, timber, fish, pork

INDUSTRY

Metalworking, machinery and tools, light electrical equipment and fittings, textiles and footwear, technological instruments, woodworking, construction materials, processed foods

MAJOR EXPORTS

Timber and wood products, machinery and equipment, metals, textiles, foodstuffs

MAJOR IMPORTS

Machinery and electronic equipment, chemicals, fuels, vehicles, beverages

MAIN TRADE PARTNERS

Export: Lithuania, Russia, Estonia, Germany, Sweden, and United Kingdom
Import: Lithuania, Germany, Poland, Estonia, Russia, Netherlands, Finland

WORKFORCE

990,000 (2017 estimate)

UNEMPLOYMENT RATE

9 percent (2017 estimate)

CULTURAL LATVIA

Holy Trinity Church
Located in Liepaja, the baroque-style Holy Trinity Church was built between 1742 and 1758. It is home to a gorgeous pipe organ that was once the largest in the world. Today, the church takes part in the international Organ Music Festival every September.

Ventas Waterfall
Known in Latvian as "Ventas Rumba," this beautiful waterfall along the Venta River is the widest in Europe. It is about 360 feet (110 m) wide and about 6 to 6.5 feet (1.8 to 2 m) tall. The nearby town of Kuldiga is known for its historic architecture.

Freedom Monument
The Freedom Monument was erected in Riga in 1935. It represents the struggle against and victory over the Soviets and Latvia's eventual independence. Flowers are often laid at the base of the monument in remembrance of the struggle.

Gauja National Park
This national park in Vidzeme was established in 1973 and is Latvia's oldest and largest national park. The Gauja River that runs through the park also lends its name to it. Some activities that people enjoy are canoeing, hiking, sightseeing, and bungee jumping.

Latvian Ethnographic Open-Air Museum
Visitors to this museum on Lake Jugla can enjoy over one hundred reconstructions of various buildings constructed between the 1600s and 1930s.

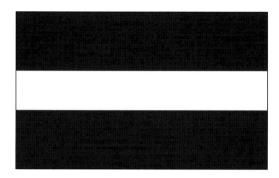

OFFICIAL NAME
Republic of Latvia

FLAG DESCRIPTION
A half-width white band runs through the middle of a maroon background, forming three horizontal bands.

CAPITAL
Riga

POPULATION
1,944,643 (2017 estimate)

BIRTHRATE
9.7 births per 1,000 Latvians (2017)

MAJOR ETHNIC GROUPS (2017)
Latvians: 62 percent
Russians: 25.4 percent
Belarusians: 3.3 percent
Ukrainians: 2.2 percent
Poles: 2.1 percent
Lithuanians: 1.2 percent

RELIGIOUS GROUPS (2006)
Unspecified: 63.7 percent
Lutherans: 19.6 percent
Russian Orthodox: 15.3 percent

MAIN LANGUAGES
Latvian is the official language. About a third of citizens speak Russian at home.

LITERACY RATE
99.9 percent (2015)

IMPORTANT HOLIDAYS
New Year's Day (January 1); Good Friday and Easter (March/April); Labor Day (May 1); Ligo Vakars (June 23); Jani Diena (June 24); Independence Day (November 18); Christmas (December 25); Boxing Day (December 26); New Year's Eve (December 31)

LEADERS IN POLITICS
Janis Cakste—president (1922—1927)
Gustavs Zemgals—president (1927—1930)
Alberts Kviesis—president (1930—1936)
Karlis Ulmanis—authoritarian leader (1934—1940, not a constitutionally elected president)
Guntis Ulmanis—president (1993—1999)
Vaira Vike-Freiberga—president (1999—2007)
Valdis Zatlers—president (2007—2011)
Andris Berzins—president (2011—2015)
Raimonds Vejonis—president (2015—present)

TIMELINE

IN LATVIA	IN THE WORLD

2000 BCE
Proto-Balts, forefathers of the modern Latvians, settle in Latvia.

116–117 CE
The Roman Empire reaches its greatest extent, under Emperor Trajan (98–117).

1206–1368
Genghis Khan unifies the Mongols and starts conquest of the world. At its height, the Mongol Empire under Kublai Khan stretches from China to Persia and parts of Europe and Russia.

1237 CE
German knights unify Latvia under the Confederation of Livonia.

1530
Beginning of transatlantic slave trade organized by the Portuguese in Africa.

1558
Ivan the Terrible invades Latvia.

1721
Russia defeats Sweden in the Great Northern War, regaining control of Latvia.

1789–1799
The French Revolution.

1873
The first National Song Festival is held, part of Latvia's first National Awakening.

1914–1918
World War I.

1918
Latvia proclaims national independence. Fighting with Russian and Germany continues.

1920
Soviet Russia signs peace treaty acknowledging Latvia's independence.

1934
Prime Minister Karlis Ulmanis seizes power.

1939–1945
World War II.

1940
Soviet Union removes independent Latvian government, installs a Soviet one, and absorbs Latvia as a republic of the Soviet Union.

1941–1944
Latvia occupied by the German Third Reich.

1945
End of World War II. The Soviet Union reoccupies Latvia.

1966
The Chinese Cultural Revolution.

1986
Nuclear power disaster at Chernobyl in Ukraine.

IN LATVIA	IN THE WORLD
1991	**1991**
Latvia reinstated to full independence. Latvia admitted to United Nations.	Breakup of the Soviet Union.
1993	
First independent elections to Saeima. Guntis Ulmanis is elected president.	
1994	
Last former Soviet/Russian troops leave Latvia.	**1997**
1999	Hong Kong is returned to China.
Vaira Vike-Freiberga is elected president, the first woman president in Eastern Europe.	**2001** Terrorists crash planes into New York, Washington, DC, and Pennsylvania.
	2004 Eleven Asian countries hit by giant tsunami.
	2005 Hurricane Katrina devastates the Gulf
2007	Coast of the United States.
Border Demarcation Treaty signed with Russia.	
2008	**2008**
IMF approves €1.68 billion rescue package to help Latvia ride out economic slump.	Earthquake in Sichuan, China, kills 67,000 people.
2009	**2009**
Demonstrators clash with police. Valdis Dombrovskis heads a new coalition government.	Outbreak of flu virus H1N1 around the world.
2012	
A referendum that would give Russian status as the joint official language is rejected.	
2013	
A supermarket collapses in Riga. Prime Minister Dombrovskis resigns.	
2014	**2014**
Latvia joins the Eurozone.	Russia annexes Crimea, part of Ukraine.
2015	**2015**
Raimonds Vejonis becomes the president of Latvia.	Paris Climate Agreement.
2016	**2016**
Maris Kucinskis becomes prime minister.	The United Kingdom votes to
2018	leave the European Union.
Latvia celebrates one hundred years since becoming a country.	

GLOSSARY

dainas (DAI-nas)
Latvian folk songs.

Dievadeli
"Sons of God."

equinox
The time when the sun is directly over the equator on March 21 and September 21, making day and night the same length throughout the world.

gulags
Prison camps in northern Russian under Soviet rule.

Jani Diena
Festival celebrating the summer solstice.

kekatas (CHE-ka-tas)
Carnival activities enjoyed in Latvia during the Christmas season.

Lutheran
A branch of Protestant Christianity adhering to the doctrine of Martin Luther, leader of the Protestant Reformation in Germany.

macron
A mark placed over a vowel to indicate that the vowel is long.

Martini balls
Festival food, made of peas, beans, potatoes, and hemp.

philologist
A person who studies language from both written and oral sources.

piragi (PEE-raa-gi)
Crescent-shaped baked buns filled with savory onion and bacon.

puzuri (PU-zu-ri)
Diamond-shaped chandelier decorations made from straw or twigs used at Christmastime.

Reformation
A sixteenth-century religious movement modifying Roman Catholic practices and establishing the Protestant church.

Saeima
Latvian parliament.

sauerkraut
A dish, originating in Germany, made of finely chopped cabbage pickled in brine.

solstice
A point in time when the sun is at its farthest distance, north or south, from the equator.

Stalinism
The theory and practice of communism developed by the Russian leader Joseph Stalin, characterized by Russian nationalism.

transept
Two hallways or "arms" forming the cross shape in the layout of a church.

Ziemassvetki
The Latvian word for "Christmas."

FOR FURTHER INFORMATION

BOOKS

Germanis, Uldis. *The Latvian Saga*. Riga, Latvia: Atena Publishers, 2007.

Johen, Silvena. *The Food and Cooking of Estonia, Latvia, and Lithuania: Traditions, Ingredients, Tastes, and Techniques in 60 Classic Recipes*. London, UK: Lorenz Books, 2009.

Salts, Ilmar. *A Stolen Childhood: Five Winters in Siberia*. Translated from Latvian by Gunna Dickson. Riga, Latvia: SIA Liktenstasti, 2008.

Throp, Claire. *Latvia*. Countries Around the World. Portsmouth, NH: Heinemann, 2011.

Verzemnieks, Inara. *Among the Living and the Dead: A Tale of Exile and Homecoming on the War Roads of Europe*. New York: W.W. Norton & Company, 2017.

WEBSITES

BBC. https://www.bbc.co.uk/news/world-europe-17522134.

CIA Factbook. https://www.cia.gov/library/publications/resources/the-world-factbook/geos/lg.html.

Encyclopaedia Britiannica. https://www.britannica.com/place/Latvia.

Latvian Institute. http://www.li.lv/en.

US Department of State. https://www.state.gov/r/pa/ei/bgn/5378.htm.

FILMS

Grauba, Aigars. *Dream Team 1935*. Platforma Film, 2013.

Kairiss, Viesturs. *The Chronicles of Melanie*. Mistrus Media, 2016.

BIBLIOGRAPHY

"Dziesmusvetki: The Song and Dance Celebration." https://dziesmusvetki.lv/en/about-the-celebration/the-song-and-dance-celebration.

Kalnins, Mara. *Latvia: A Short History*. London, UK: Hurst Publishers, 2015.

Kasekamp, Andres. *A History of the Baltic States*. London, UK: Palgrave, 2017.

"Latvia Begins to Overhaul Its Healthcare System." *Xinhuanet*, September 26, 2017. http://www.xinhuanet.com/english/2017-09/26/c_136637701.htm.

"Latvia Forest Area." Trading Economics. https://tradingeconomics.com/latvia/forest-area-percent-of-land-area-wb-data.html.

LIAA. http://www.liaa.gov.lv/en.

Lumans, Valdis O. *Latvia in World War II*. New York: Fordham University Press, 2006.

Mersom, Daryl. "Reclaiming Riga's Soviet Architecture." *Citylab*, August 14, 2018. https://www.citylab.com/design/2018/08/reclaiming-rigas-soviet-architecture/567287.

Nagy, Peter, Phillippe Rouyer, and Don Rubin, eds. *World Encyclopedia of Contemporary Theatre: Volume 1: Europe*. Abingdon, UK: Routledge, 2013.

North, Michael. *The Baltic: A History*. Translated by Kenneth Kronenberg. Cambridge, MA: Harvard University Press, 2016.

Plakans, Andrejs. *Concise History of the Baltic States*. Cambridge, UK: Cambridge University Press, 2011.

Smith, David James, Artis Pabriks, Thomas Lane, and Aldis Purs. *The Baltic States: Estonia, Latvia and Lithuania*. Abingdon, UK: Psychology Press, 2002.

Ventspils. https://www.ventspils.lv/eng.

Verzemnieks, Inara. *Among the Living and the Dead: A Tale of Exile and Homecoming*. New York: W. W. Norton, 2017.

INDEX

INDEX